What Happens When the People of God (the Church) Pray

The Rev. Dr. Gary W. Exman

WestBow Press books may be ordered through booksellers or by contacting:

WestBow Press
A Division of Thomas Nelson & Zondervan
1663 Liberty Drive
Bloomington, IN 47403
www.westbowpress.com
844-714-3454

Because of the dynamic nature of the Internet, any web addresses or links contained in this book may have changed since publication and may no longer be valid. The views expressed in this work are solely those of the author and do not necessarily reflect the views of the publisher, and the publisher hereby disclaims any responsibility for them.

Any people depicted in stock imagery provided by Getty Images are models, and such images are being used for illustrative purposes only. Certain stock imagery © Getty Images.

Scripture quotations marked NIV are taken from the Holy Bible, New International Version®, NIV®. Copyright © 1973, 1978, 1984 by Biblica, Inc.™ Used by permission of Zondervan. All rights reserved worldwide.

Scripture quotations marked NKJV are taken from the New King James Version. Copyright © 1982 by Thomas Nelson, Inc. Used by permission. All rights reserved.

Scripture quotations marked ESV are from the ESV Bible® (The Holy Bible, English Standard Version®), copyright © 2001 by Crossway Bibles, a publishing ministry of Good News Publishers. Used by permission. All rights reserved.

Scripture quotations marked KJV are taken from the Holy Bible, King James Version.

Scriptures quotations marked GNB or GNT are from the Good News Bible © 1994 published by the Bible Societies/HarperCollins Publishers Ltd UK, Good News Bible © American Bible Society 1966, 1971, 1976, 1992. Used with permission.

Scripture quotations marked ASV are taken from the American Standard Version Bible.

ISBN: 979-8-3850-2184-0 (sc)
ISBN: 979-8-3850-2185-7 (e)

Library of Congress Control Number: 2024905607

Print information available on the last page.

WestBow Press rev. date: 07/09/2024

WESTBOW
PRESS®
A DIVISION OF THOMAS NELSON
& ZONDERVAN

Where two or three are gathered together in my name and pray, I will hear
their prayer and come and heal their land.

Do not be downhearted, sad, discouraged, or lost. Why? We are blessed people to have the God of all gods as our Savior and Father.

CONTENTS

INTRODUCTION

This is a compilation of prayers and teachings on prayer, including personal prayer stories about powerful answers to prayer that is through God, by God, and for God. This book is intended to be used in a professional, preaching way, through personal study, to bring forth powerful testimonials.

Never forget what the church is. It is not buildings. It is the people of God building relationships with people who do not know God, to help them know and love God in Jesus. "The Lord is my strength and my help, so of whom shall I be afraid?"

The underlying verse for this book is "The effectual fervent Prayer of a righteous man, (or woman) avails much."

It seems to me that God is waiting on us to do something. I think I know what it is—*pray*. He wants us to be ready for His plans. So let us get ready by preparing ourselves and our churches, and then help others to trust Him.

The underlying truth is that "the Church Grows when the people of the Church cry out to God for their Soul and others souls. Thus the Soul of all Churches and the lost people of the world can and will be saved."

The End Is Near

Since I was very young I have heard many preachers say and preach these very words: "The end is near." My memory goes back to the 1940s. Since I was a young preacher, I have believed only God knows that answer. Why?

He knows all.

He is God.

He is in control.

He is our only Hope.

He only can save us.

He says, "Trust and obey me."

There are serious problems in this world, and we must, as citizens of this, God's world, start to stand up, push up, pray up, trust up, and train up. He tells us He has our backs, so let us trust Him.

God is waiting to hear from us. If we do not ask, why would He need to answer? "Ask and it shall be given to us. Seek and we will find." He wants to hear from us just like, in marriage, our spouses want to hear from us. "Let our requests be made known to God."

https://www.facebook.com/100002904211078/posts/3603795936393845/?d=n

CHAPTER 1.

Prayer: Salvation

Here are scripture passages related to the power of prayer in salvation:
Search me, God, and know my heart; test me and know my anxious thoughts.
see if there is any offensive way in me, and lead me in the way everlasting.
(Psalm 139:23–24 NIV)

Be still and know that I am God; I will be exalted among the nations, I
will be exalted in the earth. (Psalm 46:10)

But God chose the foolish things of the world to shame the wise; God chose
the weak things of the world to shame the strong. (1 Corinthians 1:27)

To live is Christ. To die is gain.
How can you find a way to God? Yes, He is and always will be out there waiting for your call to
Him. Start with a sincere call to Him in prayer.
Then read the Word.
Then go to the nearest church.
He is waiting for your call.
If fewer than half the people in the world believe in prayer, we who believe in prayer must urgently
and faithfully preach it, teach it, and practice it. Will you join me by practicing prayer together in our lives?

The Power of Prayer in Salvation
It all began spiritually for me when I was a five-year-old boy living with my parents and older
sister. We had just moved to Columbus, Ohio, from my birthplace of Chicago, Illinois. I did not know a
thing about what churches were. I somewhat remember that my mom and dad did at least say to me that
they believed in God. We recited the "Now I lay me down to sleep" prayer.
Then my sister visited a church near our home. The next night, the preacher visited our home and
invited us to church. I did not really know what a preacher and a church were until I got there the next
Sunday. After that first visit, we attended every Sunday morning, Sunday night, and Wednesday night.
I quickly learned much about God and Jesus. As a six-year-old, I "went forward and knelt at the altar to
pray for Jesus to come into my heart and become my Savior."
What a day that would be,
For the total life changes in me.

And those changes made in my life,
Which, through prayer, meant giving up all childlike strife.

So what a day that would did become,
Released from the grips of sin, yes, gone, the total sum.

I received as my Savior the God of Grace,
And it all changed even more than the look on my face.

Praise God from whom all blessings flow.

From the moment of my commitment to Jesus, my life changed forever. I learned to pray. I found out that God heard my prayers and answered them according to His will and purpose. I also learned that not only could I talk to God, but He also talked to me. From that beginning, God called me to be a preacher. That also happened when I was still six, and it stayed with me, leading me on a long journey through childhood and teenage years. Many times my faith was tested; I had numerous ups and downs. Yet through those years, I deep down found solid faith in Jesus. I confessed my sins regularly and kept my faith.

I graduated from high school, and the next two-and-one-half years were very difficult. My calling was strongly tested. Through many growing-up struggles, I never forgot who I was and where I had come by faith.

In 1958, I went, as a seventeen-year-old, directly into a four-year college program. I majored in sociology at Ohio State University. Within two school years, I had received two academic dismissals. I was not quite ready for the rigors and discipline of college.

I felt I had failed my childhood calling to preach. I knew that United Methodist ministers had to have four years of college and three years of seminary to be ordained. I felt helpless, like a failure before God. For the next year and half, I stumbled around with my life, working various odd jobs. Still, I remembered my calling.

On Christmas Day 1960, I awakened with the assurance that God wanted me to join the United States Air Force. On January 3, 1961, I found myself in basic training in San Antonio, Texas. I decided that night, in an open room with sixty beds and fifty-nine other young airmen, that I had made a *big* mistake. In desperation, I did the only thing I knew I could do. I prayed to God to get me out of the scary mess of military life.

Well, almost four years later, God got me out just about when my enlistment was up. I had spent three years in Germany as a top-secret radio operator. During those three years, God put me in ministry as a lay helper in the base chapel during my free time. I met some great airmen and soldiers who were also serving their military obligation there. I especially became fast friends with several young men like me. We banded together by praying and ministering with the chaplains on the post. We held Bible studies and attended church services. I won my first convert to Christ while teaching a Sunday school class of ten-year-old boys. The boy who accepted Jesus as his Savior was the son of one of the non-commissioned officers who was serving there with his family.

Many other converts beyond that ten-year-old boy were won to Christ as our team of prayer warriors worked together, praying, teaching, and encouraging those kids and also the German kids who came to our chapel to learn English and in the process found Jesus as their Savior.

God used those three years as a great preparation for my next fifty-seven years of ministry for God and His Church.

Another great time of ministry only lasted three weeks. It started abruptly around 9:40 a.m., on the day of infamy since called 9/11. The world stopped for about three weeks. We, the people of God, found ourselves ministering on the phone, on the streets of our small towns, in farmers' lanes, in train stations, in airport terminals, and in church buildings. As pastors all over the world, we mentioned that our doors were open 24/7. My church and thousands of other churches all over the world experienced overflowing Sunday services. On Saturdays, Jewish synagogues were full. But, just as it abruptly as it had started that 9/11 morning, it ended. Life essentially returned to everyday, busy conditions.

Many of us who preach prophetically said that the 9/11 period was a wake-up call for the end times. It was our chance to change our ways and turn wholly to God.

But here we are, some twenty years later, losing interest in God. This is seen in the rapid decline in church attendance due to the pandemic. More than 1.3 million deaths were caused by the plague of COVID. Church online became popular, with good and bad results.

This pandemic had been prophesied, and the loss of interest in God too. We need to call back the gatherings of the people of God to pray and preach the, it may be, last hope of Jesus once again.

The Asbury College so-called revival spontaneously started in 1950 in the small town of Wilmore, Kentucky. It happened again in 1970 and again in 2023. Each time it lasted several weeks on the campus and simultaneously spread over the country.

Preach out, pray up, and prophesy on, people of faith and God. The times are ripe for revival, which can be lasting.

> Blessed are they that hunger and thirst after righteousness: for they shall
> be filled. (Matthew 5:6 ASV)

God works for the good of those who Love Him. (Ephesians 2:10)

Nobody wants to die, but the Bible makes it clear that "there is a time to live and a time to die." COVID-19, which happened in the winter and spring of 2020, devastated the whole world, reminding everyone of the frailty of life. Preachers preach about Jesus, who gives eternal life. I chose the hope in Jesus a long time ago. Have you yet? You can confess Him as Savior today. Just ask Him in your heart to save you. He assures us that all who call upon His name will be saved.

Life is great while all is going well. If we learn to trust in and obey Jesus, then no matter what is happening or will happen, we will have Him always as our Savior. He has our backs and takes us through it all, good times or bad times. He is our Rock and Salvation.

Is an individual's prayer for salvation heard by God? Yes, if God knows that prayer is earnest and sincere. God answers that prayer by gloriously giving that individual eternal salvation.

During COVID-19 and the many devastating tornados that struck six Southern states in the United States in 2020, literally many millions of unchurched people turned on to the electronic-media churches. And from that turn, listening to the gospel being preached, thousands accepted Christ as their Savior, and the great revival of COVID-19 to Christ 2020 started. Praise God!

> The Lord God is—
> A great God
> A grace God
> A gracious God
> A glorious God

> A generous God
> A good God
> A giving God
> A gratitude God
> A grand God
> Praise be to God!

After COVID-19 devastated the world, the doors of Americans' homes began opening. People ventured out, and like a groundhog in February seeing a shadow or the sun, many of these people were seeing the Son of God. They were reminded of the Christ opening the doors of the tomb. Those who, in their hearts, saw the Son, saw hope.

The truth of life is that God is in control of this life and eternal life, which is salvation. As the Bible says, He is "the Way, the Truth and the LifeH ".e also is "the Author and Finisher of our faith, hope and love."

> Living, He loved me,
> Dying, He saved me,
> Buried, He carried my sins far away
> Rising, He justified freely forever.
> One day He's coming,
> Oh Glorious day, Oh glorious day.[1]

The champion of all champions in the world of spirituality, and most certainly all areas of this life, is the powerful presence of prayer, which ultimately leads us through salvation to the life to come. "Be still and know that I am God" (Psalm 46:1 NLKV).

Fifty years ago, the Menninger brothers from the Mao Clinic wrote the book *Whatever Became of Sin?* Today we still ask the same question, for the inability to identify sin as sin is still prevalent and mostly more so. First, what is sin? It is a willful transgression against God. There are not small nor big sins. Sin is all sin and transgresses equally from God's truths. We must reidentify it for the twenty-first century and preach boldly against sinning. Will you join me?

"Have mercy upon me, O God. According to your loving kindness; According to the multitude of Your tender mercies. Blot out my transgressions. Wash me thoroughly from my iniquity. And cleanse me from my sin" (Psalm 51:1–2 NKJV). The power of salvation is in confession of sin and belief in God through fervent and honest prayer.

When our dog Mi Mi was one year old, she easily got distracted from what we had taught her about "going outside." A noise, another barking dog, the smell of food—any distraction and she was off, forgetting what she had gone out to do. The same thing happens with us as Christians and our focus in life, which is to do good and serve the Lord with gladness. One little distraction and we are waylaid by selfish desires, lusts, and many other personal fantasies. God, help us to focus only on You and Your world being saved.

When a virus like COVID-19 is in the world, it is on everybody' minds. It preoccupies the families who have already lost loved ones and those who have infected friends and family. On the other side were the nurses in a Southern state who, upon hearing the cry for help in New York City, jumped on a plane without hesitation, forgetting their own chance of infection to help others in need. Here also are the new

---

[1] Doug Stockton, retired UM pastor.

technologies used by churches to reach out and preach, teach, and evangelize. Prayer will never stop. Prayer is the greatest avenue for reaching out.

"The Lord is my light and my strength, of whom shall i be afraid?" He helps me to lead the unsaved to Him who is the light and, yes, the way.

What is sin? It is willfulness of our own wills not to do God's own holy and perfect will, which substantiates the beginning of our salvation. He shows in the Old Testament and the New Testament how we can find His hope.

I say to the people of God, or the church, "Go, my people, enter your rooms and shut the doors behind you: hide yourselves for a little while until his wrath has passed by" (Isaiah 26:20).

Whatever month and year in which we are reading this, may we make it the month of prayer for those who are not saved by the blood of the Lamb. May we help people find the salvation of their souls in Him and only Him.

Why is not the word of good news out for all to hear? He is the Lord God over all other supposed, false, and ungodlike gods of this world. He is the One above this world, who came through His Son to bring faith and hope for all.

Prayer changes our lives. Prayer challenges all evil that is against us with the power of Jesus the Christ, the Son of the living and forgiving God.

A two-pronged prayer that is a great prayer is "Bless the Lord, oh my soul, and all that is within me bless His holy name." It is never too late to find salvation by praying to our Lord Jesus the Christ. Just start now. Confess your sin and believe in your heart. It is so simple that even a child can find Him in this prayer. If you desire salvation, just believe in Him. You will receive it through the power of God.

The love of God is patient and kind, generous and gracious, giving and good. It comes through prayer too, and by His power.

Here is a list of spiritual words for a saved person:
- Prayer
- Praise
- Purity
- Perfection
- Presence
- Power

Remember that the Lord will give us what we pray for in Him. But the Lord can also take away what we pray for if we turn our backs and go away from Him.

I do not pray as I should. Probably no one does. So let us together commit to more daily prayers.

Both of our children and all six of our grandchildren were saved at home around the kitchen table. First was our son, and then our daughter. Later came our first four grandkids, and finally our last two grandkids in their parents' homes.

Even among those of us called "the people of God," life goes down and then up again. When we pray in faith, whether it is a down or up time does not really matter, for both come and go. It is up to us how we handle them.

In this time of crisis and distress, I give all of you my prayers and love through the love of God, which is in Jesus Christ our Lord.

Prayer brings forgiveness of the soul, peace in the heart, and grace for one's life. Yes, the Lord is good, all the time.

Prayer saves the lost from sin and death. Prayer brings them to salvation through Jesus and His righteousness.

As Christians we have life over sin and death, through victory in Jesus Christ.

Prayer has a profoundly powerful tool at its center. Faithfulness, to those who pray, comes from that power in the center, who is the God of the universe.

Just as I am, I come to you, Oh Lord. For You are my Lord and King, my Savior and God, my Teacher and Friend.

We are all sinners who need salvation from those sins. We get salvation by asking Him to forgive us and cleanse us.

Prayer is our lifeline to God through the hope in Jesus Christ that we have and always will have. Praise be to God.

Welcome to the way, the truth, and the life, which is in and through Jesus Christ, the righteous and holy One.

A prayer of praise to God comes after being forgiven of sin or having a victory over a problem in one's spiritual life. "Lord, thank You for helping me whenever I called upon You and Your name. You heard my call and answered from heaven. You came down to me and into my heart. You saved me and followed that by changing me."

Prayer changes unrepentant people to repentant people, who then, because of their changes of heart, begin to care for others. They try to win these others from unrepentant to repentant through the same kind of prayers that they previously prayed.

I cannot get over that Jesus gives free eternal life to me through free salvation. To make it work, He offers me the great blessing of the mind of Christ and the wisdom of Solomon. Wow, what a package deal! Thank you, God.

Tell those you meet that you are always thinking about the Lord Jesus Christ. Then ask them to think about Him too.

What a sad commentary it is that one person has the ability to take evil and use it on another person to destroy them, and sometimes many others too, in just a few short seconds. God help us to use His power of prayer in us to have victory over that evil in the name of Jesus Christ.

With God, all things are possible. Yes, there are no impossible situation in His world. Here is a chance for you to trust Him. Pray now to Him, and He will hear your prayers. God guarantees that He will hear and answer your prayers. Now! Today!

Let people in trouble know that the Lord is good. Let them know that He cares about them and their troubles and will help them.

Have you been saved? Have you been to Jesus for His cleansing power? Are you washed in the blood of the Lamb? When you do praise God, you can praise Him from whom all blessings flow and praise Him for all creatures here below.

Prayer is for the churches to help the lost find Christ and hope through salvation. Then they will have eternal life.

Prayer is great all the time. Through prayer, we find out God knows us. He always shows us this by His love and salvation.

Prayer does change lives, families, churches, and governments. Ultimately prayer brings individuals to salvation. Prayer brings hope of finding salvation. But salvation is not all, for in it we can also have grace, truth, and love.

The power of prayer in faith and hope through Jesus for eternal salvation is the most important prayer ever to pray. God is our blessed Savior and Hope. He is our Father and our Master. We can have Him through prayer.

Are you on the plan of salvation that leads to heaven and everlasting life? Get on the plan by believing in your heart and then confessing with your mouth. With your words, proclaim His Word. Believe and confess; this leads you to a place in heaven.

Happy is the prayer of a believer for the salvation and everlasting life of an unbeliever. Prayer can move mountains, change thoughts, and even change lives by turning sinners to salvation. All these changes can only come through God's love.

My only hope in this life comes through salvation in Jesus Christ, His love, and His righteousness. This salvation provides me with eternal life in heaven. All is the result of prayer and grace in Jesus. God is God: goodness, salvation, grace, peace, purity, friendship, trust, and truth.

Prayerfully direct your thoughts to God. Ask Him for forgiveness, and He will hear and give you forgiveness and everlasting life. He or she who begins with salvation and then carries it on to the end of life through much prayer will receive eternal life. Please pray and then pray some more.

He is the God of salvation. Jesus is the one and only true way. You do not come to the Father but through Him.

Blessed be the name of the Lord. Jesus, Jesus, Jesus: sweetness is His name. "His name is wonderful, Counselor, the Almighty God, the everlasting Father, the Prince of Peace." and He even saves us to the uttermost."

The Lord God Almighty is powerful and strong, yet humble. He gives salvation through His gracious love to make us perfect in Him. The Lord is everlasting, all powerful, and all loving. Follow Him through salvation all the way to our heavenly home and eternal life.

The prayer for salvation helps the church to win the lost. It helps those who are saved to find hope in His eternal life. Blessed be the name of the Lord, for He brings hope and salvation for the whole world.

There is a time to live and a time to die. Blessed be the name of the Lord, for He is good and gracious. In this life, He offers us salvation and eternal life. God is real, and He offers us freely salvation and eternal life.

Prayer is the avenue that leads us to the feet of Jesus. We have a seat there forever through salvation in Jesus Christ our Lord.

Through salvation in Jesus Christ our Lord, we inherit the mind of Christ. He becomes our life and thought. He gives us love for our family, our churches, our country, our government, and this dangerous world to pray for.

We have all committed sins against God. His birth was the beginning of us finding forgiveness of sins, so every day in our belief is Christmas and Easter. He was born miraculously and lived to die for our sins and come back again for us.

Pray in private and in public. Pray positively and purely. Pray purposefully and powerfully. Our purpose is to trust that our prayer will bring people to salvation in Christ Jesus our Lord.

Prayer brings faith in the hope spring that leads people to the saving power of Christ. The Lord is my and your Rock of Salvation.

> But because you are stubborn and refuse to turn away from your sin, you
> are storing up terrible punishment for yourself. For a day of wrath is coming
> when God's righteous judgement will be revealed. (Psalm 2:5)

I Bless the Lord Who gives me counsel; in the night also my heart instructs me. (A prayer from the heart of a Blessed Warrior)

I have set the Lord always before me; because He is at my right hand, i shall not be shaken. (Psalm 16:7–8; another prayer from the heart of a Blessed Warrior)

Pray daily and get the rewards for doing so. God will show you through those prayers that love will abound in you and will also come to the others you are praying for, in salvation and truth.

Prayer—if you prepare yourself body, mind, and soul—will bring great divine intervention to others when you pray for salvation for them and their loved ones.

Prayer helps in getting you saved. It also helps make you a kinder, more pleasant person. Try it. You will see immediate results.

The handwriting is always on the wall during times of crisis. This world, when it is in a big mess, needs a plan from spiritual leaders. What will be your plan? Through your prayer to God, He will help you develop a plan for you and your church. Pray to move forward with a process in evangelism through inspiration in Christ to begin that powerful movement of revival.

Another Testimony about Prayer and Salvation

I was a part-time young pastor servicing what was called a two-point charge (two churches) while studying full-time to earn my AB degree, majoring in sociology, at Taylor University in Upland, Indiana. At one church, there was a middle-aged mother who was concerned about her mom and dad. They were in their late sixties and great people, but not saved. We started praying for them as a church. Since they owned a farm right beside the church property, it was easy to stop by from time to time to visit and pray with them too. Upon sharing with them, I learned whenever there was a community need, they dug deep in their pockets and shared to meet that need.

One day I explained to them that good works were great, but they really needed to accept Jesus as Savior in order to get to heaven. Social sharing of money and gifts was great, but salvation in Christ was the only way to find Jesus.

After that talk, the man and his lovely wife bowed down and accepted Jesus as Savior and Lord. The next Sunday I baptized them.

A few weeks later, I got an urgent call that the man had had a heart attack and died in his home. When I got to the home about sunset, I was starting to pray with the family inside when someone ran in from the yard and told us what all who were outside had seen: a shooting star had rushed into the yard from deep out in the sky. Then, after landing, it had turned and rushed back to the heavens. We all believed it was one of God's angels coming to pick up the man's soul and take him home to be with Jesus.

Needless to say, a few days later, in a packed church for the man's funeral, I could rejoice with the family and friends that if this man had not accepted Jesus a few weeks before, then, no matter how good a man he had been, he could not have been saved. He needed the Savior to get to heaven. God had sent an angel to take him home as a blessing to us all. I have never since experienced such power of the angels seen by so many in God and His wonder.

Wonder

'You must be born again'.
My mind is clear.
My heart is strong.
My knees are bended.
My focus looks forward.
My spirit is God-centered.
My prayers are heaven-sent.
My life is seeking Christlikeness.
Will you join me?

'Oh, who will come and go with me?
I am bound for the
Promised land.'
Trust and obey and thousands of you
Can go with me.

God
Reigns over us
Is righteous over us
Revives us
Renews us
Redeems us
Redirects us
And more …

CHAPTER 2.

Prayer: Forgiveness

We start with a group of my personal thoughts on prayer and forgiveness.

What is the church other than 'the people of God praying, preaching and teaching, 'what can wash away my sins, nothing but the Blood of Jesus? What can make me whole within? Nothing but the Blood of Jesus.' My new book, *What Happens When the People of God Pray?* Out by Christmas!

> Prayer
> totally changes our hearts,
> transforms our souls,
> strengthens the community,
> Brings together our marriages and families,
> Gives hope to our world.
> "He lives, Christ Jesus lives today."

The name of Jesus is above all names, above all humans and angels, above all kings, and above all life. Trust Him. He can be your Savior and Lord as He is mine.

The message from the Word is clear: "Repent and be baptized every one of you in the Name of Jesus Christ."

What is the church other than 'the people of God praying, preaching and teaching, 'what can wash away my sins, nothing but the Blood of Jesus? What can make me whole within? Nothing but the Blood of Jesus.'

Among the seven last words through which Jesus showed forgiveness while He suffered on the cruel cross were these: "Our Father forgive them for they do not know what they do" (Luke 23:34).

"But I tell you who hear me: love your enemies, do good to those who hate you" (Luke 6:27). Jesus forgives us our sins, and He pleads with us to forgive those who have hurt us, hurt our loved ones, hurt our church, or hurt anyone and everyone around us. We are to forgive those who have offended at a dastardly level, and those who have maimed us mentally or spiritually.

We love Him because He first loved us.

> For God so loved the World that He gave His only Son, that those who believe in Him shall not perish but have everlasting life. (John 3:16)

> The eyes of the Lord watch over those who do right, his ears are open to their cries for help. (Psalm 34:15)

How to show forgiveness and love is to pray. (Philippians 1:3–4)

I thank my God every time i mention you in my prayers. I'm thankful for
all of you every time I pray, and it's always a prayer full of joy.
Death and life are in the power of the tongue; And they that love it shall
eat the fruit thereof. (Proverbs 18:21 ASV)

Watch your tongue, for what you say comes from the heart.

What should one do when one sins as a saved person?

- Do not just try to forget it.
- Ask for God's forgiveness.
- Thank Him.
- Ask for strength not to do it again.
- Praise Him for His forgiveness.

Testimonies and Stories of Forgiveness in Prayer

I remember when I was about nine years old, I went down to the candy store and shoplifted an item priced at fifteen cents. This was the 1940s, and there were no hidden cameras, only the watchful eye of the owner of the store. I got out of the store without being caught. I instantly knew I had committed a sin against my mom and God by stealing that item. I knew that if Mom found out, she would kill me.

So I went home crying and confessed to my mom. My shock was she did not kill me, as I had been sure she would. Instead, she forgave me. Wow, what a relief!

From that terribly powerful encounter, I found out my mom was somewhat like Jesus. Why? Because she had forgiven me just as Jesus had forgiven me when I was a six-year-old. Both experiences taught me about forgiveness of my sins.

But the experience was not over yet. Mom told me that I had to confess to the store owner and pay him for the item. My childlike thoughts told me that confession would lead to a stint in jail. Those were the thoughts going through my little mind. I still vividly remember the whole encounter.

The very, very tall man—I am sure he was at least seven feet tall—bent down to my level and actually forgave me. He accepted my late payment for the item and told me to never, ever do that again. And I have not in the seventy-plus years since. Yes, I learned again that God forgives. Even people forgive, no matter how wrong you have been.

This experience started my lifelong journey of loving others unconditionally. I discovered, as a small boy, that this was God's way of life. "Do unto others as you would have them do unto you ",the scriptures say. Through prayer, I know the love of God through a most powerful understanding—the power of forgiveness.

In April 2020, this understanding was brought to the world's attention with the announcement of a new book, *The Coming Great Awakening*. Just twenty years ago, one of the greatest preachers of the twentieth century, Dr. David Wilkerson, the author of *The Cross and the Switchblade*, had predicted that a great pandemic would come to the world, with an epicenter in New York City. This prophet preached about the coming pandemic and several other events that have since come true. Wilkerson gave that prophecy twenty years ago at the United Methodist Congress on Evangelism. I was there, as well as more than a thousand other ministers. He prophetically said the pandemic epicenter would go around the world and lead to another Great Awakening.

Then, in April 2020, this world revival began. Preachers saw it happen and preached salvation and hope all over the world. But after just a few years, the revival disappeared. People went back to living for self, as they had before. We need not stop praying; we need to intensify our use of prayer, as it is the hope for ourselves, our families, our churches, and our world through Jesus Christ our Lord.

"Forgive them for they do not know what they are doing." This was said by Jesus as He was hanging on the cross for doing nothing wrong—yes, absolutely nothing. Yet, as a painful personal answer for us, He forgives them. This was one of the most difficult experiences Jesus had.

He said while He was ministering that not only should we love His Father with everything we are and will be, but that we should love our neighbors as we love ourselves. That is fine for neighbors we like, but what about neighbors we do not like? OK, Jesus, I get it. We must love them too. And He makes it harder, for we are to love them as much as we love ourselves.

"The steps of a good man are ordered by the Lord, and He delights in his way. Though he fall, he shall not be utterly cast down; For the Lord upholds him with His Hand" (Psalm 37:23–24 NKJV). This will all come from a person asking forgiveness and giving forgiveness.

I am *still* focused on my Savior and God through His Son, Jesus the Christ. Are you? If you are not, then believe in Him by confessing your sins to Jesus in your heart. Then proclaim that with your mouth in His name. Text me, and I will pray for you.

Forgiveness to those who have spoken evil against me has been hard, but it is "the way, the truth, and the life."

A prayer for forgiveness is powerful. There are three points to learn:
- It always works when it is of God.
- It always works if it is based on truth and trust.
- It never fails.

One power of a prayer of forgiveness is that if we believe in that power, it works. Throughout my whole life, I keep learning more and more about it. Here I am at age seventy-nine, and I feel like I need to learn more. God, teach me, today and in the future, more and more about prayer and how to forgive through it.

Does prayer make your day? It is my only hope of forgiveness for me, my wife, my kids, my grandkids, people in my churches, and people all over our country and our world.

Remember, prayer has no weakness. Through prayer, you can even forgive those who abuse and hurt you.

Here are seven ways we show our love to God:
1. Love the Lord God with all your heart, soul, mind, and strength.
2. Love yourself.
3. Love your spouse and family.
4. Love your neighbor as yourself.
5. Love your church (the people of God).
6. Love your country.
7. Hope for eternal life with God in Jesus. Yes, it all starts with Jesus giving us His forgiveness of our sins. Then we must forgive others for offending or hurting us.

We should all remember that if we don't forgive, we cannot be forgiven. The Word reminds us that if we withhold forgiveness, we are in danger of having forgiveness withheld by God, thus endangering our hope for eternal life.

In the time of forgiveness, let us remember our enemies as well as our friends. Yes, forgive all who have offended, both those we love and those who have given us pause and sadness.

As I write this, Holiness Week is coming up very soon. Let us start today, right now, to seek holiness unto the Lord. Being holy as He is holy will give us a much better love, Christ's love, to serve others in all of our and their time of need, with prayers.

Bless the Lord, Oh my soul, and all that is within me, Bless His Holy Name.

For the Spirit God gave us does not make us timid, but gives us power, love and self-discipline. (2 Timothy 1:7)

The most expensive liquid in the world is a tear. It's 1% water and 99% feelings. Think before you hurt someone, because it is better to forgive than to hurt.

The Lord is good and plenteous in mercy. He is the Forgiver of all forgivers. Have you found His forgiveness by just asking Him?

In a period of crisis, it is time for men and women of God to rise up in powerful prayer and loving sharing. This is a time, whenever and wherever we go, to trust in Him. His forgiveness to us has come and will go on in the future.

Prayer does change lives, families, churches, and governments. Why? Because prayer brings change to the individual, his or her family, his or her church, and even his or her government. These changes come through forgiveness by the power of prayer.

Remember that Jesus told his disciples to obey the rules of government and to pray for those who govern. Forgive the government for wrongs and encourage the leaders with forgiving prayer.

Who in the whole world could ever help me? Only One, or as we call Him the only One, that being Jesus the Christ. He forgives me of my sins, then cleanses me, and makes me whole and makes me Holy in Him, who is "holy, holy, holy! Lord God Almighty! Early in the morning, our song shall rise to thee."[2]

The Lord is up there in the heavenly places, watching over all we do and judging all we say. He will ultimately judge the just and the not-so-just (unjust). Are we ready for His forgiveness? Though we do not deserve it when He does forgive us.

Always turn the right way—to God's way, which is always right. That way you will never go the wrong way or do the wrong thing. The right way is to be forgiven by Him and to in turn forgive others.

Because you, only you, forgive you, then forget what you have so grievously done by erasing it away as far as the east is from the west.

Need a direction change in your life? Remember, God will put you in His direction, which will always be right. You will give forgiveness to others and be forgiven by Him.

It is much better to give love to others than to demand they forgive you when you have wronged them.

Life is mostly good, but there are many bad bumps along the way. I can only handle these bumps by keeping on the road to heaven, which was given to me by His love and forgiveness.

In the time of trouble, who in the whole world could really help me? Only One could, He being the Lord Jesus Christ. He is my Forgiver, Savior, and God.

The Lord is up there in the heavenly places, watching over all we do and judging the just and the unjust things we do. Are we ready for His judgment day?

Forgive those who most powerfully use and abuse you, for you, as Jesus did, can most powerfully forgive them.

Prayer gives us an attitude of love and forgiveness to and for others. Share that spirit of prayer regularly.

When we pray and win over evil, evil loses its power over us, one way or another.

---

[2] "Holy, Holy, Holy! Lord God Almighty!" Traditional hymn, lyrics by Reginald Heber (1826).

As we pray in the Lord's Prayer, "Our Father who is in Heaven." What does that mean for the world?

- God is there.
- He is over the world and rules it.
- He is our Hope and Savior.
- He will take us there forever.
- He eternally loves and protects us.

A Personal Experience

I had cataract surgery on both eyes a while back. After the surgery, I could see 20/20 without glasses or contacts. When you are forgiven of sin by Jesus, it is like spiritual surgery on your life. You start seeing differently, like 20/20 vision.

After forgiveness, prayer and praise show us how forgiveness has worked in our lives. Why? Because this new life gives us peace, joy, and purity. Is there anything more important than that?

Some say words like "To forgive or not to forgive, that is the question." But that is not right. The Bible teaches that it is always right to have a spirit of forgiveness through the power of prayer.

Pray daily for yourself and for those who need to be saved. We all need prayer and need it now. Pray with me, will you?

There is nothing greater in this life than a prayer life that leads us—and many others—to the afterlife, which can be eternal life in Jesus Christ.

Watch and pray. Stay focused on what to say in prayer for people who have gone the wrong way. We should forgive them for what they have done at first. We can follow up by lovingly helping them with much prayer and care.

Prayer with love is needed frequently, sincerely, generously, and with goodness. Stick with it, especially toward those who have hurt you and have not told you they are sorry.

More Testimonies and Stories on Prayer in Forgiveness

In my many years of ministry, I had to learn to unconditionally accept and forgive people, usually ones in my church, who had hurt me deeply with verbal abuse about me and my ministry. It was through prayer that I learned how to forgive people who had been spiteful toward me.

I remember a time when a person of leadership in the church was working against my ministry very strongly. It was very difficult for me to love that person, because that person was stopping the church in its spiritual growth. While that was happening, that person became very sick, an illness that led to intensive care. I went daily to pray for that person's healing, knowing that, when healing came, that person would be back to working against my ministry. But because of the unconditional love God had given me, I prayed daily for that person to be healed, to come back, and to berate me for the way I was leading the church.

That person got well and lived two more years. And indeed that person continued the quest of trying to stop my ministry. The only way I survived was disciplined, unconditional love. How many times has God had to unconditionally love us when we impede His work? That is what forgiveness and love are all about.

Another person in another church I served came to church regularly. For whatever reason, that person would not greet me or respond to me. Every week, I persistently greeted that person. Later I heard that person was having surgery. When I went to the hospital, that person responded to my visit with much joy and appreciation. When that person returned to church a few weeks later, recovered from surgery, I was once again greeted with a cold shoulder. Until I moved from that church, the shunning continued. I continued treating that person with loving kindness. Prayers from my praying friends and family kept my unconditional love intact in both of these cases.

Agape love, taught and preached to me from childhood, focused me on unconditional love. This is what holiness is all about. The love chapter in the New Testament is my favorite on this subject: "Love is patient and kind, never jealous or envious or proud."

CHAPTER 3.

Prayer: Trust and Obey, Holiness

Here are Bible verses that teach us how to pray so we can trust through obedience, leading to deeper faith called holiness.

Trust and obey for there is no other way.

Humble yourselves under the mighty Hand of God …casting all your care
on Him for He cares for you .(Hebrews 11:1)

And now some testimonies and stories about what trusting and obeying God and growing to holiness leads to in one's life.

Trusting and obeying God in Christ are the only way to find God's love. It's how we become close to Him and find His holiness in our lives. It all starts with humbling ourselves to Him. And yes, we must humble ourselves if we really want to be under the hand of God. Receiving Him and His power is the greatest challenge of all for those who have taken the first step and accepted Him as Savior. Following salvation, we must let Him take over our lives in a holy way.

I must admit this has been one of the hardest undertakings in my eighty years of life. I have ended up more like Peter in the Bible narrative, who was, in his early life, such an up-and-down follower of Jesus. My walk with God has taken too many turns: off in side directions and then back to the straight and narrow for a while again. God, forgive me and help me again to trust and obey You.

I heard a powerful football story from the University of Eastern Michigan. Their season was just getting ready to start. Two seniors had been friends for their first three years on the team, one on a full scholarship and the other in his fourth walk-on year. He was probably going to start at his favorite position, but there were no one-year scholarships left, though he deserved one. The scholarship player asked if he could give his senior year scholarship to his walk-on friend; his family would pay for his final year. Scripture alludes to "loving our neighbor as we love ourselves." Another passage talks about giving one's life for another. The annals of war are filled with soldiers giving their lives to save their brothers in arms, their teammates.

Our Savior gave His life on a very cruel cross to give those who ask forgiveness eternal life.

Here are a few of the great spiritual leaders of the twentieth century—some of them still living. Their work with God and His Word, and their prayers—together with my prayers and those of many prayer warriors—have helped me.

The Reverend Dr. E. Stanley Jones
The great world evangelist of the twentieth century was the Rev. Dr. E. Stanley Jones, who

preached and lived "surrender to Jesus "daily. In my opinion, he was the greatest evangelist in the Methodist movement. I have read all of his twenty-plus books and attended many of his religious retreats. I have been guided by his intellectual and spiritual teachings.

The Reverend Dr. Harold Dutt

I remember with fondness and respect the pastor of my childhood and youth, the Rev. Dr. Harold Dutt. He lived and preached holiness all his life and guided me from boyhood to adulthood.

Coach Floyd Eby

Coach Floyd Eby was a teacher from Coldwater, Michigan, who was also a basketball and football coach until the age of fifty. Then he retired to be a lay evangelist, mostly to youth, all over the USA. He wrote five books about youth and youth evangelism while preaching and teaching Jesus in hundreds of schools and churches, including four of mine. He won thousands of youth to Christ.

Dr. Timothy Clark

Dr. Timothy Clark is the pastor of First Church of God, Columbus, Ohio. He has been a spiritual leader to me and showed me how to lead a church by being both humble and strong. He is a great brother and friend and has been a great influence on my life.

Rhett Ricart

As co-CEO (with his brother Fred) of a large auto dealership in Columbus, Ohio, Rhett Ricart stands out as real Christian prayer warrior and friend. I saw him go through the lowest and the highest of days. He always stood strong. He and his brother raised two of their sons to follow as co-CEOs. Their dealership has been a leader in sales growth for Columbus. I have developed several of Rhett's spiritual qualities in my life. He is a deep-praying man.

Mark Thompson

Mark Thompson came into my church in Columbus, Ohio, and stayed for about five years, giving his great spiritual expertise and financial support, which were much needed during growth times. As the son of a Baptist preacher and a part-time missionary in Haiti, he worked together well with me. Thank you for your love and support, Mark. You are a praying man, and your prayers and spiritual guidance have been great.

Chuck and Lyndsey Casey

Chuck and Lyndsey Casey came into my life about twenty-five years ago when they came to my church. I married them at Chuck's bedside after he had been sick in the hospital. They gave great spiritual help to my church as powerful prayer warriors as well as great friends.

Clair and Nancy Harting

Clair and Nancy Harting helped me to emerge as a full-time pastor in Convoy, Ohio, many, many years ago. My first three years there were rough because of a powerful person who was running the church, overriding the will of pastoral leadership. Assisting Clair was Bob Wiseman. After more than three years of spiritual warfare in that church, things smoothed out and greater things happened. I served there for thirteen years. I became a pretty good pastor, prayer warrior, evangelist, and prophet. Thank you for getting me going, Clair, Nancy, Bob, Warren, and my five prayer warriors.

Stan and Norma Miller

I helped Stan and Norma Miller get back to personal relationships with Jesus in the twenty-first century. They in turn have greatly helped me grow in the faith and grow as a prayer warrior. Thank you, Stan and Norma.

Dr. Harry Denman

Dr. Harry Denman was the lay head of evangelism of the UM Church. I really got fired up by his story. He preached in many towns all over the country, and his life dramatically changed when he went to Hattiesburg to preach at a revival. He stayed in the local hotel and preached at the local church.

On his last morning, planning to witness to the young, he was riding in the elevator and noticed a different operator. He asked, "Where is the young man who has been running the elevator all week?"

The operator answered, "Sir, haven't you heard? My friend committed suicide during the night."

Denman said that, at that moment, a huge sadness enveloped him. He had planned to witness that very morning to that operator, and this sad news canceled his plan.

He told the audience that his life turned around that day. He became the one-on-one witness many saw and knew so well. He prayed to God for forgiveness and received that forgiveness. Yes, in spite of the failure, he had a great future as a witness. Literally thousands were won to Christ because he learned the hard way to conduct himself in obedience to the Holy Spirit.

My life changed because of Denman's testimony that day. I began praying with strangers in stores and at events wherever I went. Sometimes God would tell me to turn in a different direction than I had been going in, and thus led me to a person in need. I learned to expect these turns in the "wrong" direction—which ended up being the right direction.

One time, upon turning off at the rest area, an emergency vehicle swished by me before I could park. I was prompted to follow it. Where it stopped, there was a man in deep pain. While EMTs were getting their equipment out, I knelt and prayed with the man and saw immediate relief in his expression.

Another time, I came out of a theater and encountered a man who had seemingly died. I prayed for a few minutes over him. An emergency squad came and revived him. I heard later the man lived.

Another time, I was in the restroom at a rest area. A man took the stall next to me. I heard him gasping, and I asked how he was doing. I immediately prayed for him, without laying hands on him, and he instantly felt better. He told me he had had a catheter in all night and was on his way to the next town for his wedding ceremony. I have thought many times since about his wedding night.

There are powerful, tragic examples about forgiveness and the holiness that follows. Consider the unbelievable attack on our country on 9/11, which most of us will never forget. Thank you to my two favorite teams, Ohio State and Dallas, with their renditions of the national anthem and many other forms of remembering the anniversaries of this horrible attack. Pray for America to turn again to God, as my church did daily after 9/11.

I must include a word about the many faithful women I met in my ministry who were prayer partners and warriors. Women are the backbone of prayer. In my first book, *Get Ready, Get Set, Grow*, I highlighted five older ladies whom I met weekly in prayer meetings. They took our ministry into deep prayer. In every church I have served in since, I have recruited women like these five prayer warriors to pray for all the church's needs.

Here are some of those powerful moments of my life when I mostly stood alone on the Word of God and the power of prayer. "The effectual fervent prayer of a righteous man, or woman, brings (availeth) much." I don't think I was that righteous, but God really honored my meager efforts to be, at least, partly holy.

An example of standing up happened about twenty years ago, when I was serving a four-year term as president of the United Methodist Council On Evangelism. A minister came up to me after a seminar I taught and asked me to come to her church in a small town in Texas. She told me about what was going on five miles outside her town, on a hilltop. I had seen some of what she described in TV news reports.

After I arrived at her town, we decided to drive out to the location she had described. We pulled up at an iron-chained gate that closed off a dirt road winding up a large hill. I got out of the car, held up my hands, faced the hill, and prayed from the depths of my soul. "Lord, in the name of Jesus, free those preteen and teenage girls from that evil man and his brother. Lord, only you can do this, so make it happen. In Jesus's name I pray."

We left the location with no apparent changes seeming to have happened. Nothing happened at the hilltop during the weekend. The preaching conference was held at her church, and on Monday I went back home to my ministry.

I had not been home too many days when a major news flash said the sheriff and social workers in that area of Texas had taken over the compound on the hill and were processing the girls, adult women, and children there. The evil man and his brother had been tipped off about the police raid, and their whereabouts were unknown. I once again prayed that these girls would not be placed in foster homes but reunited with their mothers. God heard girls' prayers and mine. Today they are living in community on that hill. Since then, that evil man has been arrested outside of Los Vegas, booked, convicted, and sentenced to a lifetime in jail.

I know my prayers were not the only prayers offered for those girls, but the act of urgently praying was what God wanted me to do. Will you join me and go to pray where He leads you?

Another leading of God sent me to pray at the large hotel in New Orleans three weeks before Hurricane Katrina happened.

"I will go where you want me to go, say what you want me to say and be what you want me to be dear lord."

Church buildings were closed on March 15, 2020, which was a very important day called the National Day of Prayer. We, as Americans, found out that day what was and what was not the church. The people of God are the real church. Nobody can close their outreach as long as they trust and obey God in what He wants them to do, which is witness and evangelize.

The power of a mind that is dedicated and focused on serving Christ is what we need to pray for and seek. Include the wisdom of Solomon, and you will win for Jesus the battles ahead.

During the pandemic, we became basically prisoners in our homes. Over the years and ministries, I have been in many incarceration facilities to see prisoners from my communities. I also have ministered to many guards in my churches. When COVID-19 came, my prayers for them changed.

Prayer works by phone, by email, and in all ways for others near and far. I prayed in person, face to face, for fifty-eight years with great results. Now in my eighties, it is almost all by phone and email. That works wonders too. I pray with every doctor, solicitor, friend, and robocaller. Pray on, all warriors. Trust and obey. It is time to rise up—men and women, boys and girls of God. We can become prayer warriors of God and bring revival to a fearful world.

Now is not the time to be weary, down, or discouraged. God is waiting for you to cry out with praises and petitions in prayer as you trust and obey.

On March 15, 2020, the president of the United States told us to be safe from the coronavirus by holding a national day of prayer against the virus and practicing social distancing. So we did social distancing to defeat the virus. We became the real church, which is the people of God, by practicing spiritual closeness to defeat sin and bring revival and holiness.

In any time of crisis, remember, "God is in His Holy Temple, so let the earth rejoice." Here in America we have hundreds of thousands of prayers always going up. In a time of crisis, it's possibly double that amount. God answers all those prayers. His answers are according to His will, not ours.

What is sin? It is willfulness. It is our own will to do wrong by not following His will. It is His will for us to obey His own holy and divine will, which makes us children of God. Thus we are the church.

Take a whole month and make a commitment to stress prayer in your life. Remember, there is much to pray about, such as people, places, problems, and your own personhood. So it is always time to pray.

Prayer is given to believers for seeking the mind of Christ. Its sole purpose is to evangelize and do good while combating evil. On the other hand, Jesus in our hearts and souls is our comfortable confirmation of seeking holiness.

A prayer warrior prays in the belief that, in God's timing and will, they will receive His answers. A prayer warrior prays for our leaders in the world, the nation, the state, and the churches.

Why don't we prayer warriors get the word out? He is the Lord God over all other supposed gods, which are false. He is the One God Almighty, the most powerful of all. Praise Him from the housetops, our marketplaces, and even from our church buildings. Praise Him all of us, his children, for God is love. "Because the Lord is my Shepherd, He gives me everything I want and need" (Psalm 23:1–2, Exman translation).

God supplies all a prayer warrior needs. He is our Shepherd, and we are His sheep, following Him. We trust Him to take care of us. Our God is great, good, gracious, generous, glorious, and full of gratitude for our love for Him.

Prayer is great. God is good. The Holy Spirit is powerful. Love is and always will be victorious to those of us who know Him, love Him, and are called to His purposes.

Prayer, praise, and peace brings purity to your heart and holiness to your soul. There is nothing more important to your life in Jesus Christ.

Look into church history and see how it undeniably works. A few fervent people, humbled in powerful prayer, can lead a mighty force for God and His works. Look into church history and see the work of those who have gone before. They trusted and were obedient to Christ our Lord. They were fervent prayer warriors. They led a mighty force of saints who changed the world in many of the past generations.

You who are standing in the need of prayer can know that we, the people of God, are praying for you. We hope you are finding forgiveness and love through Him.

A possible way to holiness is to have the peace of God come upon you through prayer. Then saturate yourself in the Word of God. Prayer brings life abundant and eternal life forever.

Oh, how great are your works, and even greater is Your holiness, oh God Almighty!

Once we seek God and His holiness, we find His mind and Spirit in our souls and hearts, so we are better prepared to help those who are in great need.

I am seeking more of the mind of Christ and the wisdom of Solomon. Will you join with me and do the same? God bless us together!

Powerful prayers that are urgent, sincere, heartfelt, and God-centered are heard in heaven. Yes, God hears and answers those prayers.

It is always a joy to teach seminars on evangelism and prayer. We need more of these. Along with worship, they are the lifeblood of the church and the people of God.

Life can change in a moment, such as when horrific storms or national disasters happen. Prayer is there for our asking. Prayer brings hope and grace in times of trouble and need. A Christian filled with prayer is a Christian worth knowing and trusting as a friend in Christ who can influence lives.

Prayer has a place in anyone's and everyone's hearts. Have you got prayer in your heart? If not, put prayer in and let God help you get closer to Him.

Jesus is on my mind. Jesus is my heartbeat and soul. The way to Him is to trust and be obedient to Him by praying daily to Him.

Let us pray for a huge revival in America and around the world by the end of the next ten years. Let us trust and be obedient in praying together for this to happen. "The Lord is Risen, yes, the Lord is Risen indeed." Remember, He promised us He will come to us again and take us away from sin and death. That will come to us through trust and obedience and be forever.

Love those neighbors living within a few miles and those living thousands of miles away. Love them like you love yourself.

"As. For God, His way is perfect. The word of the Lord is proven; He is a shield to all who trust in Him" (Psalm 18:30 NKJV). Yes, this is a taste of holiness. Love the Lord with all you've got: body, mind, soul, and spirit.

God is good even when things around you are bad. Just keep prayed up and He will work all things together for good. We know Him and are called according to His will and purpose.

Pray abundantly for the spiritual storms of life. Do not forget the storms of disaster that plague our world—it seems that such disasters are a daily occurrence.

Prayer is answered by the people who are trying to be holy and truthful and who have sincerely thought out that prayer in love.

Blessed be the name of the Lord, for He is great and gracious, slow to anger and plentiful in mercy for those who trust and obey Him.

Never forget the Lord, for He is God.

Christ is Number One above all and over all. He takes our all if we trust and obey Him with all our hearts, minds, and souls.

God is good even when I am not so good. God is good all the time. He is especially happy when He sees that I am doing good by trusting Him.

Holiness can only be found by much prayer and surrender to Almighty God in Christ Jesus, our Lord and Savior.

Prayer and praise brings peace and purity which is holiness. There is nothing more important to do in a day.

He is the wisest God of all gods, who presents us before His grace and glory in holiness. He is able to keep that which I have committed unto Him against that day by trust and obedience.

My most important message? Keep praying every day. That can only be done by trusting and obeying. Prayer works when you value it with your life. Remember to trust and obey, for there is no other way. Pray helps us with the problem of learning obedience and thus having full trust in the Lord. An obedient follower learns what real trust is.

There in *no* time when you cannot pray. You must never quit praying. We are always to trust and obey, and in obedience to pray, pray, and pray some more.

I cannot emphasize enough prayer's value, importance, integrity, grace, strength and truth. Your life and the health and hope of your church rely on prayer. Prayer is full of trusting and obeying God.

God is great all the time. He knows us and always show His love to us if we just trust and obey His teachings.

On my birthday, I am making a new commitment to a better diet. I'm also committing to learn more about what it means to trust in the Lord always and to believe in the Lord in the now.

God is good, great, and the Greatest. Let us trust and obey Him now and forever more—and more still.

Jesus is the One to trust. Jesus is the One and only One whom we must follow by almost perfect obedience.

Is there another One? Is there another way? Is there another belief? Is there another truth? Emphatically no, no, no, *no*! Trust and obey.

Prayer is the straight and narrow road to heaven. Don't take a curve on the path, for you will lose your way.

Whom can we trust? Whom should we obey? In God we trust. It is God we obey. Blessed be our God. He is the wonderful God whom we love, obey, and trust.

There is a name I love to hear: Jesus, Jesus, Jesus. My desire is to trust and obey Him.

If we do not trust God with all our hearts and believe God with all our minds, how can God believe and trust all of our prayers? Think about that.

"What is truth? "Pilate once asked centuries ago.

In the same century, Jesus said," I am Way, the Truth, and the Life for no one comes to the Father but by me." Thus, when preachers preach in this twenty-first century, they must teach His truths and obey those truths in their daily lives in order to find the answer to the question Pilate asked and Jesus answered.

Prayer leads us to a great trust and an unusual obedience in and through the Lord.

When you pray, do so as your heavenly Father would have you pray. Pray by showing Him your beliefs by trusting and obeying His teachings.

Prayer warriors are:

- committed only to God
- convinced God is the only God
- controlled only by His Spirit
- concerned mostly for the lost
- convicted to trust and obey Him

Obedient and trusting prayer goes hand in hand with a joyful and peaceful heart.

I believe in the Father, the Son, and the Holy Spirit, who are the one and only true God. I trust Him and obey Him only.

There is a time to live and a time to die. By trusting and obeying God, we can live through the times of life and death with eternal hope. The Lord is good and gracious. In life or death, we are in His hands when we trust and obey Him. Yes, there is no other way but to trust and obey.

Is Jesus real? You bet He is. I have banked my life on trusting that He is and being obedient to Him.

Prayer is the avenue that leads us to the seat of our everlasting God through Christ. We walk that avenue with obedience and trust in Him.

Having the mind of Christ for one's life can help one to obey and trust Him enough to follow Him in helping others to find Him too, through prayer and witness.

God is better than good. He is and always will be the greatest and only true God.

- He loves everyone unconditionally.
- He is greater than any other so-called gods.

- He defeated, is defeating, and will always defeat Satan.
- He forgives all who sincerely repent of their sins and who trust and obey Him through prayer.

Churches can only grow—and I cannot emphasize it enough—when the people called t"he church" lift up their value, importance, integrity, grace, strength, and truth on the life and hope of their fellowship. It comes by obeying and trusting Him through their prayer in holiness.

When you pray, do so as your heavenly Father would have you pray. Pray by showing Him you believe. Trust and obey Him in holiness, and He will hear your prayers.

The power of prayer receives a great boost when the prayer reflects the power of trust in and obedience to Jesus. Trust in the Lord and obey His teaching through your prayer life and yours daily living.

Prayer works when one commits to it with one's life. Yes, it works when one follows one's Creator by trusting and obeying Him.

Thank you, Jesus, for reminding me that you are just a prayer away.

—Juanita A. Exman

What a difference a lot of prayer makes! The people of God have the power to win the lost. What a difference a heap of prayer daily makes in the life of you and your church.

God is in the spiritual business of saving souls and answering prayers in His will and time.

Prayer brings hope, which leads to faith and ends with much love and eternal life.

Why pray? Why *not* pray? Here are five reasons why people do not pray:

1. Nobody has taught them the worthiness of the power of prayer.
2. They have had a bad experience with prayer in the past.
3. They are not motivated about the importance in praying.
4. They do not really believe in God.
5. They have not experienced miracles in prayer.

Here are five reasons why I do pray:

1. I pray for recommitment to my faith and trust.
2. I pray to remember my call to preach at six years old.
3. I pray to prepare myself in the morning for a new day.
4. I pray for my family and church.
5. I pray for the lost, the poor, the needy, our country, and our military.

Prayer is answered when it is truthfully honest and when the praying person is trusting and obeying their hope in the Lord.

A good mindset is a good attribute to have in life. A good mind is a good attitude toward living. But I believe a great mind only comes when God gives one the mind of Christ and the wisdom of Solomon. This attainment only comes when one, in prayer, learns to trust and obey.

Those who go deep in prayer will find the depths of God's truth, integrity, and love.

More Testimonies and Stories about the Power of Prayer

The star quarterback of the New Orleans Saints, in the fall of 2019, referenced Romans chapter 13. He interpreted the chapter as saying the greatest command is to love the Lord God with your all and to love your neighbor, near and far, as you love yourself. Bring Your Bible to School Day was coming up, and he praised the idea and day. He received a firestorm of hate from the American news media and liberal voters. His witness to his faith in God for the things of God was a great profile of his courage and his trust in his Savior, Jesus.

Early in my life I was blessed to have prayer warriors as my Sunday school and Bible study teachers. These teachers were very prominent in my young life from grade school through high school. There was a huge emphasis on the power of prayer in their teachings. Even in early grade school, God was teaching me how to pray to Him. Likewise, in those early years, I learned how to hear God's voice. I was not a perfect kid at all, but, more than I understood, God showed me He had a purpose for me through my call to preach from Him. His plan for my life was filled with turns and twists. But in spite of those difficult times, He kept His power for teaching me to hear His voice powerfully and understandably in an ongoing way.

Let me stress it again: I was not perfect in any way. But let me stress for you too that it is Christian commitment to holiness that God expects. When one is sincere about striving for holiness, God keeps hearing. It takes continuous discipline and instruction.

The guidance of my pastor and the seminars I attended—led by the great evangelist, preacher, and teacher, Dr. E. Stanley Jones—showed me that the ultimate road to holiness was one word, as Jones preached so eloquently: "Surrender."

I am still striving for holiness in my eighties. In seeking daily surrender, I have some days or even weeks of spiritual neglect. I fail miserably in my spiritual life. I "pray up "after God spiritually reprimands me. I survive and start the daily surrender oover again.

If you have failed, as I have failed, several times in your life, please stop now and pray for forgiveness. Start anew with surrender. Strive again for holiness and the presence of God's Holy Spirit in your life. It all involves trust and obedience.

> Trust and obey,
> for there is no other way
> to be happy in Jesus
> but to trust and obey.

I wish I could teach you an easier way to learn and discern how to hear and know that we are to "be still, and know that I am God", as the Word of God teaches. Use these simple steps to come to an understanding. Learn to listen to Him and then follow Him as He tells you what He wants you to do.

- Be still. It might take several days of trying to really understand what being still means. But God will teach you as you go.
- Pray. The Word says, "Ask and it shall be given you. Seek and you shall find. Knock and it shall be opened unto you."
- Believe and call out.

It is easy to lift up a prayer. Anybody can do it. What is difficult is to have a daily, sustained life of fervent prayer. It is important to remember in this life to lift up the powerful scripture passage, "I can do all things through Christ who strengthens me."

Praying does not work. Did I write that? Yes, for only "effectual, fervent prayers by men, women, and children avails much." Let us be fervent and pray much.

Prayer always works, so never stop. There is no other way than prayer.

Grace, when it is given to us from God, gives us eternal life and everlasting joy. "Ask and out shall be given you."

Truth and its co-word *honesty* are the higher ground over the popular, evil word *lie*. Let us remember that Pilate once asked, "What is truth?" Jesus countered that He was and is truth. Good will always overcome evil, so praise God.

Think about the people of the world during COVID-19. The virus hit hard and head-on. The

Word says, "God is Good, yes, God is not good for the moment, or for an occasion, but God is good all the time whether in good or bad. So God Bless always.

If we want to know what is going in the world and what can, will, or could happen, remember that it is our Father's world. Read His sovereign words in His Word.

What is happening in this world? Cheating, lying, deceitfulness, godlessness, sexual sin, assault, and loveless evil. But God is still watching. What can we do? Pray, trust, and love.

> My mind is clear.
> My heart is strong.
> My knees are bended.
> My focus looks forward.
> My spirit is God-centered.
> My prayers are heaven-sent.
> My life is seeking Christlikeness.
> Will you join me?

CHAPTER *4.*

Prayer: The Church

We are the church, the people of God, and you too are the church if you have accepted Jesus as your Savior. The church proclaimed, "My God shall supplies all, yes, all our needs according to His riches in Glory through Christ Jesus."

      With God, the past and the future are both now.

      It is hard for us, in our finite minds,

      to understand God and His infinite wisdom and love.

      Remember, He is in control as Redeemer and Savior.

      Let us only trust Him.

      Prayer

      totally changes our hearts

      transforms the soul

      strengthens the community

      brings together our marriages and family

      gives hope to our world.

      "He lives, Christ Jesus lives today."

What is the church other than the people of God praying, preaching, and teaching? What can wash away my sins? Nothing but the blood of Jesus. What can make me whole within? Nothing but the blood of Jesus.

We need to develop more emphasis upon reaching men in our churches by developing more men's ministries. When we do so, women will support these efforts wholeheartedly. Men are needed to work with women to lead the church to victory in Jesus.

With God, we have possibilities. Scripture proves it with many verses. Here are two:

      With God all things are possible.

I can do all things through Christ who strengthens me.

More Testimonies and Stories about the Power of Prayer

When I was about eight years old, my mother took me under her tutelage about tithing, which is the way God planned for the church, or the people of God, to reach out in ministry.

In the late 1940s, my parents gave me a dollar-a-week allowance and told me that ten cents was tithe. My mother asked our church treasurer to give me a year's worth of envelopes. Once I got those envelopes, each Sunday I put ten cents in the offering. I could spend forty cents on candy. Fifty cents went into my bank account.

This was the prayerful, thought-out method my parents used to help me so I could learn to tithe. They used the same system of tithing from their own weekly earnings. When I was fourteen, I made ten dollars a week as a newspaper delivery boy .I automatically put one dollar in the offering, used four dollars for fun spending, and set aside five dollars for savings.

Each Christmas, I received more than one hundred dollars in gifts from my one hundred customers, and I gave ten dollars of it to the church. By the time I was seventeen, I had about five hundred dollars in my savings account, which paid for my first, unsuccessful year of college.

Later, during my four years in the US Air Force, it was easy to do the same with my military paycheck. Based on what I had learned from my parents' teaching, I was able to give to my military chapel my tithe.

Back in civilian life, God began to speak to me about real, deep giving. Ten percent was my tithe, which I owed to God through the church. The tithe was my Christian obligation to give back to God 10 percent of what He had given to me. But God was also guiding me to give another 10 percent of my gross earnings as my gift to Him.

When we married, my wife and I agreed to this dual commitment. Over the rest of our years of ministry, we committed 20 percent of our salaries to the church. We were probably one of the best-giving units in our churches.

I have not shared this in a "look at us and what we do "way, but to share what you can do in a most powerful way to make real your commitment to Christ and His church. He does not want just 10 percent or even 20 percent from our lives. He really wants us to give 100 percent. So my question to myself, and really all of us who are the people of God, is this: Are we committed wholly and holy to Him and His church, of which He is the Head?

Yes, giving your tithes to the church is God's way of sustaining the buildings that the body of Christ erects to meet for worship and training so the living body of Christ, the believers, can go out to win the lost. Jesus said a great deal about faithful giving.

The church buildings and ministry cannot work without the believers' commitment to give. That giving only begins with the tithe; it often means much more than a tithe. This church is really the people of God.

Yes, "power corrupts and absolute power can corrupt absolutely." But remember, God is the Power of all power as the Creator Almighty. Neither one nor many can ever defeat, disturb, distrust, disrespect, or destroy Him. He is King of kings and Lord of lords.

Today, with seemingly everything crumbling around us, we need something or someone solid to hang on to. There is only One who is strong and unbreakable. He is the Rock of Salvation, and He is Jesus.

Church attendance is way down. We need the power of prayer from the church once again. What are the church's strengths? Prayer, preaching, teaching, fellowship, small groups, and more. Get back to church!

Fewer people believe in God, worship, or even think of going to church in America today than were doing so fifty years ago, in percentage terms. What can we believers do about it? Pray, evangelize, preach, teach, and love. Tell the world about Jesus as Savior and Lord!

The people of God are to give of their tithes and offerings to build the kingdom of God so that the whole world can be won to Christ. So what is the people of God's one purpose that they should *never forget*? With the funding that goes out in those tithes they give, they are likewise to go out and preach and pray for the power of God in salvation. As the Great Commission says, "Go into the whole world and preach The Gospel to all."

> The church
> (The people of God)
> Need to heed
> The giving to God of 10 percent of our harvest seed,
> For thus is our purpose indeed.
>
> To give to the poor we must.
> So do not give in to your lust,
> For the result of such is a bust,
> For it is in God we trust.

Come on, church! It is our time to lift up Jesus, the Light of the World. Through us, may we let your light shine—yes, shine all over the whole world.

Come on, people of God! During the 2020 pandemic, you stood up for what you believed. You combined social distancing and protection with freedom in worship. Muslims can shout out Muslim prayers on the streets of Minneapolis for their religious holidays. So how about Christian freedom of religion? Legislators, let us be God's people with our freedoms.

I believe in the churches at large today because of five important, positive reasons that make them strong:

1. God's eternal and forever blessing
2. God's tenderly giving His church the power of prayer
3. God's people lifting up evangelism
4. God's truths in the inspired, living Word
5. God's teaching to lift up the youth, who are the present and future

The COVID-19 period in 2020 was the perfect time for evangelism. People were open, as they once were a long time ago, to hope in Christ. I said then that it would take a three-part, concerted effort: much prayer, deliberate witnessing, and meeting physical needs, all with great *love*. I urged immediate action.

Now we can look back and see if we got seriously to work.

During the riots and other lockdown tragedies, I determined that what we Christians could do was pray for God to come and make peace. Let us pray for God to come move us with His power.

Prayer has a place in sickness and in health, in bad times and in good times, in the church and wherever the people of God go.

People of God, remember: "And do not forget to do GOOD and to SHARE with others, for with such sacrifices God is pleased" (Hebrews 13:16).

In the year 2020, the battle was against the virus called COVID-19. The victory three-step was 1) believers and prayers, 2) doctors and medication, and 3) distance, clean hands, and face masks.

Rural churches and MAGA churches then had about three months of a green light to reach out to the lost. In a crisis, the lost are open to listen to the call for salvation. The people of God now need to use the phone, use texting and Facebook, use the front door (observing the six-feet rule), and use Visio preaching. The window is short-lived, maybe only a few months. Help and evangelize *now*! It is urgent! When people are open to the Word, go for it. "The fields are white unto harvest. Reap brother and sister.

People of God, the real church, don't you know? Cannot you see? It is clear to me that God has given us a green light to act. It is our time to pray and evangelize. In a crisis, we are the only hope. People who are unsaved will listen now! So let us begin. Let us start our prayer engines and go out into the fields for a big harvest of souls. They are ripe for the picking.

> If you burn down the church building and drive away all the people, you have not disturbed Christian worship at all. Keep a Christian from entering the church sanctuary and you have not in the least bit hindered his worship. We carry our sanctuary with us. We never leave it.
>
> —Aiden Wilson Tozer

The church is the people, and the leader of the people of God is the "called to preach and teach Pastor." For fifty-seven years I have been one of those leaders, and I made every effort to be out there, in the homes and in the hospitals.

The living church is the people of God. During lockdown I was isolated and praying as I wrote this book on prayer. Pray with me that this pandemic will pass, people will be healed, and millions will be born again in Jesus Christ our Lord. There is something in the air bigger than any virus.

For the church, the people of God:

> Praise God from whom all Blessings flow,
> Praise all ye creatures here below,
> Praise Him above the Heavenly Host,
> Praise Father, Son and Holy Ghost, Amen.
>
> —The Doxology[3]

Listen up, church! "If a tiny virus can do this much damage, imagine what a mustard seed size faith can do?

The church is the people of God, and the leader of those people is to be out there preaching, teaching, and praying. For fifty-seven years. I have been one of those leaders. I have gone on more than four thousand hospital visits. I've also gone into every home of my people from my churches, praying and promising hope and love.

The church, the people of God, has a habit of only maintaining the status quo instead of achieving a growth quotient in winning the lost. Let us get it right. During the 2020 pandemic, I noticed that American pastors were, supposedly because of safety precautions, unable to get into the doors of the hospitals in this country. *Big mistake.* In my experience, the prayers and The Presence I named greatly enhanced the healing process. Visits of hope and healing, and the united efforts of doctors, nurses, medication, and prayer caused miracles to happen.

There are many prayer warriors in this land—which is your land and my land, America the beautiful. These warriors rise up mightily, as a segment of the people of God, to reach out their hands of healing to the thousands who stand in need. That need is met by the heaven-felt and God-centered power of prayer.

For my healing ministry, I have always used the method of the laying on of hands—the touch of God on people who need prayer. During the COVID emergency of not touching by hand, I am lifted and reached out with my hands without touching, knowing God's power was working through the symbolism of my hands, representing the healing hands of Christ.

It is a great time for evangelism. The people of God's kingdom always have a clear path and an upper hand. Praise Jesus, the greatest Evangelist.

---

[3] Words by Thomas Ken, 1674.

Prayer is powerful to the churches that want to grow. Think what would happen to the world if every church made prayer its number one priority.

What a wonderfully marvelous God we serve and worship through Jesus Christ our Lord. Praise Him.

> Prayer is great.
> God is good.
> The Holy Spirit is transforming.
> Salvation is real.
> Life in Christ is victorious.

Today and every day, the Church Triumphant needs more prayer in front of and behind it than ever before in history. Let us pray diligently and faithfully for our beloved bride of Christ.

God is the God of His church, which is the people of God, through His hope, peace, power, love, life, salvation, and light to the world.

The rural church, which is the people of God, believes and practices prayer like no other prayer group. They also are spread all over the country. They are in every nook and cranny, so to speak, of the whole world. They are about 70 percent of all the churches. What a powerful force they are. Let us pray on, church of God.

Through the people of God, the church in prayer gives us His salvation. So whom shall we fear?

The church grows when its people become serious about the mission of the church, which is prayer and the power of evangelism working side by side in unity and faith.

As a leader of the church, I am sorry that sometimes I get things wrong. Please trust me; my heart and mind are still making an effort to correct what I write and say, and do what is right.

The Lord is good. He gives us plenty of mercy and love through the Word of God, prayers from His people, and victory in salvation.

Remember, prayer is used by God as we talk and listen to Him. From this interaction between us and God, many people can and will change for the holy good. Remember that we, the church, are the bride of Christ.

Pray for our world, our country, and all the leaders in them. Pray for the churches of the world and all of their thousands and thousands of leaders. Pray for one another.

If the church is really the people of God, individually or corporately, then the work of the church comes from those gathered to hear preaching—as when Jesus stood on a boat and spoke to the people sitting on the sand.

Since we are the church, the people of God, what can we do more than anything else? Yes, we are the hope of the world, the prayer warriors. So let us all pray together now and throughout the year. Pray, pray, and pray more.

Happy are we of the church who trust in the Lord, in prayer, and in His teachings.

Prayer is always on the Christian's mind. A Christian believes in pure, regular, and powerful prayer.

Why the people of God do not use their greatest power, prayer, is a mystery. God gives them prayer to bring survival and revival and then to win the lost. Come on, church! Survive and revive through prayer.

Martin Luther's famous hymn, "Ein in festa burg is Unser Got," is translated as "A Mighty Fortress Is Our God." We can deduce from this powerful statement that the church is most profoundly supported by God in and through His people's prayers.

The church is the people. They can meet anyplace, anytime, and in any way to make anything in and through prayer happen for Him and through Him.

The church building is primarily where people come to worship, praise, hear preaching, hear teaching, and, most of all, have a chance to accept Christ as Savior through the leadership of the Holy Spirit in prayer.

The churches are for preparation and evangelistic teaching in the Word of what prayer is. Those who have been taught use this knowledge to go into the world around the churches find the lost. That follows with bringing them to Christ and into the fellowship of the church.

The church finds its standard in Jesus Christ our Lord. He is the gold standard through the power of prayers by His believers.

Churches grow in numbers and in spirit through the power of prayer. Churches can only grow when the people want growth, starting with much prayer.

The building where the people of God meet is the worship center. The actual church is the people of God. The church is one foundation with one Founder, one future, and one faith, all in Jesus Christ our Lord. We pray to Him and believe in His divine leadership.

Church growth is a methodology to lead others to Christ through prayer, preaching, teaching, evangelism, and outreach. Churches grow when the leaders of the church begin and end with the emphasis on praying. The church will mightily grow when its people get serious about evangelism and prayer. Yes, prayer works when the church prays.

I love people and that special group of people called the church. I love both groups of them dearly and deeply and pray for them regularly.

It is time to pray for all of our sister churches, from other theologies and interpretations of the Scripture, for their ministries and growth.

C-H is at the beginning and end, and what is in the middle? U-R or "you are." So Christ is two cornerstones of the church, and U-R in the middle. You go out, witnesses for, and stand for Him and His work in prayer.

The church growth movement of twenty years ago is alive and well but is using some new titles and ideas and deeper biblical truths alongside its original, foundational power of prayer. Churches can only grow when the people of the churches want to grow and start that growth with much prayer.

The church is the one foundation that will never crumble. The church will never be discouraged, dismayed, or defeated. God will take care of us because we are the people of God.

Churches will only grow when their leaders are intentional with the following principles of growth:

- personal commitment to Christ
- personal commitment to prayer
- personal commitment to the leadership group
- personal commitment to the church growing
- personal commitment to working 24/7

Prayer is powerful to the churches that want to grow. Think what would happen to the world if every church made prayer its number-one priority. Churches grow when the people of God get a strong hold on who and what the real church is and was always intended to be—the always-growing, always-praying, and always-serving people of God. The church must use outreach and God's grace for others to find their hope in whatever time of need they are experiencing.

If going to church is just a habit or something you have always done since you were taken as a child, then that just makes you a church attender, not a Christ accepter. If you have not accepted Christ as Savior, being an attender is not the way in. At heaven's gate, only those who accepted Jesus will be invited to come through.

The ways to salvation that are common talk on the streets will not get you through the gate. It doesn't matter if your mom was a good Christian. It doesn't matter if you have perfect attendance at Sunday school. It doesn't matter if your uncle was a preacher. It doesn't matter if you're nice or generous to those in need. It doesn't matter if you live in so-called Christian America. It doesn't matter if you're respected or honest or fair. None of that matters. What matters is that you have accepted Christ as your Savior.

The church building and all its wonderful texture and artistic finery—even the cross at its center and the huge steeple on top—is not the church. The church is the people who meet there regularly to worship, hear preaching, receive teaching, and pray. The church building is where the people of God meet. They leave that building to practice their faith.

Churches must be diligent in following growth principles if the church is to grow. These principles are spiritual and biblical truths found in the Book of Acts.

Churches that want to grow need four positives: deep prayers, integrity, strong commitment, and hard work. Those churches whose leaders who go deeply into prayer will find the depths of God's truth, integrity, and love for themselves and their churches. Church growth happens when the leaders read and heed the Word through much prayer.

A few years ago, one of the largest cathedrals in the world, Notre-Dame de Paris, caught fire. But a huge cross of victory remained untouched right in the middle of the fire. Maybe this was a sign from God to show that a church building can fall, but the cross will always stand as a symbol of victory over sin and death.

Why Pray?

When the people of the churches pray, those people will receive God's grace, healing, and love.

Prayer in the churches is equally as important as love in marriage.

Prayer can stop sin on a dime.

Prayer changes a sinner to a saint.

Preachers take that to the church and preach it, as the people of the church really want that kind of preaching.

On Sundays when there is no meeting of the church, such as during the crisis of COVID-19, we should never fear. The real church, the people of God, is always alive and well, preaching, teaching, sharing, and praying. Go forward, people of God! Prayer by the church makes the people of God shine for Jesus and His love.

Prayer by the people of God has lasting positive effects toward goodness and grace in God's truth. Prayer by the people of God can lead seekers to confession of their sins and belief in God. The final results of that is salvation and eternal life. For the church, the people of God, it is never, never too late to pray and praise our Lord Jesus Christ. Start now, and do not give up or give in.

When the church, the people of God, desires to pray for something and really believes in it, the church can receive it through prayer.

> Love is patient and kind,
> gracious and good,
> great and generous,
> giving and grateful,
> but not greedy.
> Love is a guide to our lives through prayer to and by Him.

The spiritual side of strength in the church is prayer. The physical side of strength in the church is people. The church *will grow* when it is steeped in powerful, relentless prayer. Churches grow when church people, the people of God, are prayerful, caring, committed, united, biblical, and Jesus-centered.

Prayer by the people of God makes them shine for Jesus and His love. I believe in God, Jesus, and His love to lead the people of God to His hope.

Prayer can, in moments or hours, change our desires and the focus of our lives. God is in the business of changing our direction to His direction. Yes, the church needs to be a direction-changing station.

During the COVID-19 lockdowns in 2020, many of us called out, "Instead of a world in chaos, could not we be a world united in love and prayer? Lead on, people of God!"

Today the Church Triumphant needs more prayer in front of and behind it than ever before in history. Let us pray diligently and faithfully for our beloved bride of Christ.

Church buildings are very important, as community landmarks and places of worship, to the twenty-first century movement of God. But sometimes a less costly approach can be renting rather than building. Remember, the real church is the people of God. Either way, move onward and upward, people of God.

Prayer is the salt of the earth to the church. Prayer is the power and the strength of the church. Prayer is the heart of the church. So let us use it hourly.

Please remember to pray. If the people of God do not pray, then COVID-19, the churches, our government, and the world will not have the power of prayer. Start with yourself.

Remember that even if you do not go to church, but you have accepted Jesus as your Savior, you are saved, and those who are saved are the people of God.

> Because I am a believer in Christ,
> I am the church.
> And if you are believer in Him,
> You are also the church.
> Where two or three of us are together,
> We are the power of what is really the church.

CHAPTER 5.

Prayer: Blessed Prayer Warriors

Here are Bible verses that can help make you a spiritual leader and a prayer warrior:

> Humble yourselves under the Mighty Hand of God, that He may exult you in do time, casting all your care upon Him for He cares for you. (1 Peter 5:6–7)

> Now faith is the substance of things hoped for and the evidence of things seen. (Hebrews 11:1 KJV)

These two passages are great for anyone who is in any kind of personal crisis. The whole chapter of Hebrews 11 is a great list of faithful prayer warriors of God. Each of them desired only to please God. Additional references to them are in the Old Testament. I recommend the study of their examples.

Testimonies and Stories about Prayer Warriors

As I mentioned in a previous chapter, the greatest prayer warrior I have ever known was a world-class spiritual leader. In the twentieth century, he traveled the world, preaching, teaching, and praying. He was nominated and elected as a Methodist bishop. But after wrestling with that verdict, over the following night he resigned. He said that after much prayer, he humbly could not accept such a high calling. God had told him he must continue preaching, teaching, evangelizing, and praying. He did just that until his death in the early 1970s. His name was Dr. E. Stanley Jones, and his message for the whole of his personal life was one word: "Surrender."

As a teen and throughout his life he embodies that word, which meant "holiness" to him. His whole life was spent preaching and practicing holiness unto the Lord. His desire as a warrior for God was to lead anyone he met to find that kind of surrender to God in Jesus Christ.

E. Stanley Jones, with his contagious witnessing for Christ, influenced my life very deeply. I had personal encounters with him and read all of his more than twenty publications, which I studied over and over again.

When I was born, I was destined to be a preacher. I ultimately became one. I was called to preach right after I accepted Jesus as a six-year-old. God spoke to me in my heart and said He wanted me to preach.

Twenty-two years later, I was finishing seminary and making my final preparations to be ordained. One of my classmates asked me if I knew who I really was. I answered, "Of course I know who I am. I am Gary Exman." My classmate then asked if I remembered a point we had learned just a few months before as we studied Greek. The X that stands for Christ in Greek could be translated into English as Ch.

My friend asked again, "Who are you really?"

He had deduced for me the answer. The "e" is almost always silent in words that begin "ex." Since my name is Exman with the silent "e," the real beginning of me name is X, Christ. I am the X or Christ Man. I am the imperfect preacher who is a Christ Man. May there always be Christ in me to give hope to others, so they can see His image in me for His hope and glory. After fifty-eight years of ministry, I am still trying to be Christ Man.

When each year ends, we pray, asking God for forgiveness of sins past. In the new year, we begin anew, praying for victory over all sin. This is what a prayer warrior is and does.

The song says, "Blessed be the Name of the Lord." You are blessed when you pray regularly.

We are in this life, but He is far away in heaven. Never fear. Though He is there, He is near and close to our hearts. Blessed be that tie that binds us to Him.

God is in control in this world and in the world to come. God be praised. May His world reign and we not fear.

Pray, pray, pray, and pray more for our country and its leaders. Pray for our pastors and churches to take leadership by lifting up prayer and love. Christ is the Love over all loves. Remember, God is Love. We love Him with all our lives because He first loved us. Tell everyone this great truth, blessed warriors.

Righteous and holy prayer is much needed by the people of God. We know how to guide the world with our prayers and personal help. Prayer is the essence of belief and trust in God. If you really believe in God, you lift a lot of daily prayers of praise and petition directly to God.

God is great. God is good. So let us thank Him for who we are and what we are, only in and through Him. Tell everyone, prayer warriors.

We were reminded on Easter 2020 by Jesus, who is the Author and Finisher of our faith, about His work on and over the cross. He had to suffer and have faith.

What about this word "work"? It is part of the two-pronged, age-old Christian, biblical truth. "Faith without works is dead." Here is the answer to the victory over COVID-19. The doctors and prayer must have worked together to win. Looking back to Easter 2020, did we put the two together, work and faith, to get the win?

A single person can change their world. If they become a daily, powerful prayer warrior, the world around them will greatly change. Even the whole world can drastically change for the good.

As prayer warriors, we must follow prayer, which is the essence of our part of trusting in Jesus. So when a crisis winds down or is over, what will we do with our learnings from it? Try these four actions: rejoicing, recommitting, rediscovering, and reviving. Each of these actions are from God, and trust me, they work!

Many world experts say prayer does not work. But there are thousands of prayer warriors, who can show they are wrong. Shock the world by praying with me for revival and miracles. Pray on, blessed warriors.

"Blessed are the peace makers: for they shall be called sons of God" (Matthew 5:6). Pray, blessed warriors, for peace. When we bless others, we do so in the name of the Lord.

The first day of a new year is the day to rejoice as we prayer warriors begin anew, serving others and doing things in Him for them. Prayer warriors, tonight is a time to begin anew in hope and love to refresh yourself and do three things daily: pray, pray, and pray more!

For a prayer warrior, all of life can be good or difficult or even bad. But with God in Christ, life leads upward to heaven with grace and love forever in Him.

At the end of the year, take a few days to clean up the wrongs of the past and start the coming new year with a clean slate, a new hope, and a time for service to God. It is a great time for a prayer warrior to pray for forgiveness of sins past. Then, when the new year begins, pray for victory over sin and death for the new year. Pray with me.

To be a powerful prayer warrior, seek the mind that is only in our Lord Jesus Christ. His mind, which is over all minds in heaven and on earth, is really the mind of all minds. I can get a taste of this mind through much renewed prayer.

A prayer warrior needs to know six constants in praying, which God will give through discernment in ones prayer life:

1. why to pray
2. when to pray
3. where to pray
4. what to pray
5. whether to pray
6. who to pray for

When one figures these six things out, one can learn better how to pray for oneself, one's family, the church, and the world.

A warrior knows that all prayer is good. So a prayer warrior knows there are no bad prayers except self-centered, selfish prayers. God is good, and we should know to pray, for prayer is good. Seek it, practice it, give it, and do it for others.

I ask the prayer warriors to keep their belief in the power of prayer. Some have tried it and then gotten discouraged because the results were not to their pleasing. Please try again, and you will see faithful prayer works. Yes, trust God.

This is the day the Lord has made. May we all rejoice and be glad in it, and may the prayer warriors rise up in prayer.

Prayer warriors have to decide for themselves whether to activate prayer's power. Remember, not using prayer is abusing prayer. Using one's prayers and abilities brings the power of prayer to others. God is Love, and warriors praying will bring that greatest love to others.

We must learn from warriors that there is no other hope that holds our lives together, which we have in the power and love of Jesus.

Warriors, remember, Scripture says, "What you desire when you pray, believe and you will receive."

Warriors, make your prayers bold. Then God will hear and know you really mean them.

A Song for Warriors
There is power,
Power,
Wonder-working power
In the blood
Of the Lamb.

Warriors know that prayer is calming and that it affects us
At any place,
In any time,
And in any way.
Catch hold and hang on with that warm calm that will come by prayer
any and every day.

There is not anything better to do today than pray. Tomorrow, start over again with more prayer. Each day after that, make it more prayer.

I believe in God, Jesus, and love. The power of prayer brings these three together to work for the glory of God. May the grace of God, the hand of Christ's healing presence, and the power of the Holy Spirit in prayer be with you and yours. "Draw nigh to God, and He will draw nigh to you. Cleanse your hands, ye sinners, ye sinners, and purify your hearts, ye double minded" (James 4:8 ASV). This is the way to be a warrior and find holiness in Christ.

Prayer lifts up your body and your soul. It also lifts up your marriage and your family, so you can leave home for work being ready as a prayer warrior.

You who have let me know you are standing in the need of prayer, you can most certainly know I am praying.

There is nothing greater in this life than having a prayer life that leads us and many others to the afterlife. which can be eternal life in Jesus Christ.

The biggest plus in prayer is that it works 24/7, 365 days a year. God never stops listening to and answering our prayers. Though we sometimes think He is not listening, He always hears, and He answers in His timing. A prayer warrior trusts Him at His Word.

Praises are the beginning of praying, which show God our love for Him. Following praise come petitions, and then our listening quietly to Him. Praying ends with more praise.

A blessed prayer warrior is one who is called to, as A. W. Tower says, "an everlasting preoccupation with God."

Prayer has a grasp on my life. That hold has sustained me in a time of trouble and retained me when His power was needed in me—and through me to others—as the blessed hope.

We need prayer as Jesus: with full sincerity, from our deepest heart depths, with a full focus on God, and with full emphasis on God's will and purpose. Does this lead to holiness? Absolutely.

The Lord is good, gracious, and great, and we bless His holy name.

God constantly has to remind me to keep my spiritual hat on my head and use the mind of Christ that God has given me already. From the mind of Christ God has given me, I am to go out and be His warrior for His grace and glory.

Prayer has a grasp on my life. It sustains me, it trains me, and it helps me to refrain from evil. Praise God.

He is the wisest God of all other creatures, near and far. He presents us with hope and blessings in Him through His grace and glory.

The blessing and benediction above all others says, "And now unto Him who is able to keep that which we have committed unto Him against that day."

A most important blessing for your life is to keep on praying every day of your life. Then the blessing will keep on coming and coming.

Prayer is the quickest way to speak to God. The Bible is one of the best ways to hear back from God. Learning these truths gets you closer to God's love and His holiness.

Blessed be the name of Jesus. We love Him and want to bless others with His wonderful blessings. The name of Jesus, yes, Jesus, the sweetest and most blessed name I know, fills my every longing and keeps me singing as I go through life.

Prayer warriors are committed only to God, convinced God is the only One, controlled only by His Holy Spirit, and concerned wholly by wanting to win the lost. The prayer warrior believes and has peace of heart, family, church, country, and world.

Prayer warriors believe in the Father, the Son, and the Holy Spirit. That Trinity is the only true God in Jesus the Christ. The warriors have figured out this Trinity. Have you figured it out? You only do so by much prayer and reading of the Word.

I recently had both eyes operated on for cataracts and now see with 20/20 vision. When Jesus operates on our hearts, we will come out of that spiritual surgery seeing clearly as a warrior for Christ, the world, and its needs.

Prayer is very hard for those who are weak and weary, so we need to pray for them. Powerful prayer comes from those who are strong in spirit. Their power comes from the Holy Spirit, and they are often called prayer warriors. They have the kingdom of God and those they win to Christ in their sights.

Pray in private and in public. Pray positively and purely. Pray purposefully and powerfully. Pray, pray, and pray more.

Prayer for healing and holiness has a grasp on my life. It sustains me. It trains me. And it helps me refrain from evil. Praise God.

To be a prayer warrior, one must follow four practices. One must pray with full sincerity. One must pray from the heart. One must focus on God. And one must find God's will.

Prayer gives us an attitude of love and forgiveness toward others. This attitude leads us to holiness, which leads on to sharing it with others.

When we pray, we will win every time. Evil loses every time, one way or another, in the confrontation with a prayer warrior in Christ.

Who I believe in and pray to is Jesus. Yes, Jesus. Jesus is the sweetest name I know. He fills my every longing and keeps me singing as I go about my daily life. The Lord is good and plentiful in His mercy for making me what He wants me to be.

Prayer warriors start themselves with prayer every morning. That time of prayer must include prayers first of praise, then of confessions, and last of family, churches, country, and world.

I will pray any time, any day, and any way for what the Lord would have me be and say. Prayer has an abundance of love and a heap of hope to encourage us to use it often.

> Prayer works.
> Faith works.
> Hope works.
> Love works.

How do I know? Because through my trust in God and belief in His Word, I have tried all four of the necessary prayer practices. They work. God never fails.

More Testimonies and Stories about Blessed Prayer Warriors

Today, with seemingly everything crumbling around us, we need something or someone solid to hang on to. There is only One who is strong and unbreakable. He is the Rock of salvation, and He is Jesus.

As I wrote about in a previous chapter, two great influences on my life were lay evangelists. One was Coach Floyd Eby from Coldwater, Michigan. He was a Gideon, and I first heard him in a church in Celina, Ohio. From that day, I started a lifelong relationship with him. I invited him to preach in my churches and schools, first in northwest Ohio, then in southern Ohio, and last in Columbus, Ohio. He wrote five books about youth witness and evangelism and gave those books away wherever he went. He talked to people about Christ in any place and at any time. He barely slept because he prayed the night away every day of the year. This praying led him to be a tireless evangelist with a desire to win the lost.

Thousands were won to Christ by his persistence and love. He was a true prayer warrior and evangelist of the twentieth century.

The other lay evangelist who exercised great influence over my life was Harry Denman. He preached, taught, and prayed wherever he went. For years he was the head of evangelism for the Methodist church, stationed in Nashville, Tennessee. He prayed with people everywhere he met them: at dinners, on planes, and anywhere else. They kneeled together and prayed the prayer of salvation. Yes, Denman was another person committed wholly to Christ, day and night.

After he retired, I was blessed to hear him once. It was at a meeting in Nashville, Tennessee. He was asked to give a ten-minute greeting. Two quick hours later, he finished his greeting and sat down. His talk became a lifelong memory for me.

Denman slept in his office. He gave away his coats and suits to the poor and homeless in Nashville or wherever he went. He said he only needed one suit. He was truly an inspiring prayer warriors and evangelist of the twentieth century.

Without faith it is impossible to please God. (Hebrews 11:6 NIV)

> There is nothing like a warrior of prayer
> For his total purpose is his prayers to share
> To stop him you wouldn't dare
> His prayers for you went to heaven and back
> Because of his care

We should remember God answers prayers for little needs in our everyday lives as well as big needs. I remember going through a tough time with an inner ear infection and being prescribed a three-week course of antibiotics. After the antibiotics, the infection was gone but my inner ear was still blocked, impeding my hearing. I prayed on it that night.

The next day, I was driving by my doctor's office and decided to stop in. The receptionist said there was no chance I could see the doctor that day, but a week later I could. I prayed in my heart. Suddenly, she told me to wait a minute, and she went back into the inner offices. Five minutes later, she came back and said the doctor would see me after all. One half hour and an inner-ear procedure later, I left with a clear ear passage and good hearing again after three months of suffering. Yes, God hears our prayers according to His timing, will, and purposes.

CHAPTER 6.

Prayer: Healing, Victory

Here are Bible verses that show the power of prayer to bring healing victories.
And now unto Him who is able to keep you from falling, and present you before the presence of His Glory with exceeding joy and to the only God our Savior, be Glory and Majesty, Dominion and power, both now and forever more. (Jude, last 2 verses. KJV)

Humble yourselves therefore under the mighty Hand of God, that He may exult you in due time, casting all your care upon Him for he cares for you.

Testimonies and Stories about People Being Healed Victoriously through Prayer
There was a Sunday school teacher who rarely said a word as a teacher in more than thirty years of teaching teens in a church in Wheelersburg, Ohio. I was his pastor for eight years, and he was so powerful that I trusted him and his wife as the teachers of my two teen children and scores of other youth while I pastored that church.

How did he influence all those kids for Christ? By using not his speech but his actions of love. He gave every kid he met a piece of gum, followed by his never-ending unconditional love. That made him known famously in the Wheelersburg area as "the man with the gum and a smile."

Then he was diagnosed with cancer, which, over the course of five years, devastated his whole body. He fought it daily with much prayer and faith, along with much, much prayer and faith from countless others.

His answer came recently when he received his home-going. There were only ten immediate family members present at his funeral because of COVID-19. But scores of people listened to the service through telecommunications. Everyone in that area who loved the gum man, and his life knew their prayers for his healing had been answered after those five years. He continued to go to work each day and never missed his Sunday school class and church services until the very end. Now the gum man is among the heavenly hosts, passing out gum to the millions there. God's power makes the gum last: there is one piece each for all those millions, just as Jesus transformed the few loaves and fishes into enough food to feed the five thousand.

God is the greatest because He hears our prayers and heals us. Through this healing power, He shows us He loves us and cares for us all the time.

Prayer and fasting can't go wrong. They make our commitment to Christ lasting and real. They bring rejoicing and healings. Pray on, men and women of God.

If we want to know what is going in the world and what can or could happen to this world, remember that it is our Father's world. Read His sovereign words in His Word. The most important message is to keep healing in your life. Keep praying for that healing every day.

I have committed sins in my life. Finding forgiveness in Him heals me from that sin and sadness.

This is the time to build a wall around our world of prayer protection by praying in unison for the sick, the needy, and especially those who have not turned to Jesus and accepted Him as Savior and Lord. Let us warriors of prayer together surround everyone in the world with much prayer.

If prayer has one fault, it is that it does not work if it is not used. We get no results from it. No prayer means no benefits.

Prayer fertilizes the church, the people of God. It empowers the church into action for the good of God.

Our world is in need of robust healing. We need healing in our bodies, our spirits, and our souls. Remember the church, the people of God, is still open. So use your healing skills through Christ in prayer, you warriors of God.

Today I am not a fool, because the faith in God in me is greater than all foolishness.

Life is short.
Prayer is long.
God is golden.
Grace is eternal.
Love is beautiful.
And marriage is rewarding.

God is Love.
God is Love.
God is Love
To all of us, His little children.

The Lord gives and the Lord takes away, so blessed be the name of the Lord and His wonderful ways.

The Lord is in His holy temple.
Let all of us on earth rejoice.
Praise God from whom all blessings flow.

The Lord is my Shepherd,
Whom shall I fear?
The Lord is my King, my God, and my Savior.

I love You, Lord. Thank You for what You have done for me, my family, and others, giving us Your love and grace.

The Lord is my God and my Savior. He is the Savior of the people of the world, past, present, and future.

The spiritual side of the strength in the church is prayer. The physical side of the strength in the church is the real church, the people of God.

"God is our refuge and strength, a very present help in trouble" (Psalm 46:1). Yes, He is there to heal us and bless us. Blessed be His name and truth.

A great message is to pray daily. It strengthens our souls and heals those around us.

Prayer will be eternal. We will talk with an eternal God in heaven through His Son (and see Him too).

Prayer and fasting go together like marriage and family. We need both sets. Put them in unity and go for the best in your life and for the healing of others. They make our world solid with God. Bring us together, Lord, with our trust and faith in You, to see healing in the world through love.

Thank you, God, for two-way prayer.

Pray much and receive much back in return. If you do not pray, you will not get any answers from God's healing and power.

Prayer goes with worship and praise. It brings healings of the body and soul.

Prayer is the summit of all human life. It counts on everything we do and say.

Jesus is on my mind. Jesus is in my heartbeats. Jesus is my soul's desire. Through praying to Him every day, my soul is cleansed and my body healed.

Prayer is the art of any deal, and it is the real deal with God. He is in the business of making deals with people and their lives by using His deals to bring them healing victories.

Let us pray for a huge revival to happen in the world by the end of the year.

Prayer lifts up our bodies and our souls. Prayer also lifts up the world with healings of body, mind, and soul.

Pray daily and get the rewards for doing so. Try it, and you will soon find those rewards of healing and prayer.

Remember, when the church building is closed, the real church—the people of God—is all over the world, preaching, teaching, praying, and healing. The church is using electronic messaging more than ever before. As the printing press did for Luther, so electronics now have leveled the playing field more than ever before.

Prayer, when practiced regularly, is filled with abundant healings and blessings. Prayer leads to victory in emotional comfort, in sickness and health, and in sorrow and pain.

The first thing to do when waking up is give prayers of praise to God. Then pray for yourself, for your body, mind, and spirit. After that, you are ready to help others in powerful ways.

The Lord is good. He gives us hope and love in the time of trouble and need. Heal us, Lord, and blessed be Your name.

I am thinking now about the Lord Jesus Christ. Are you too?

A way to touch those around us with healing victories is to pray in public. Pray positively and purely, which leads to purposeful and powerful prayer. Yes, pray, pray, and pray more.

We need to pray as Jesus did. We will be helping others to know Him and receive His healing power in their minds, bodies, and spirits.

Since God is the greatest, it is evident He wants to give healing to His people.

Prayer and fasting lead to wholeness, healing, and holiness.

I am not ashamed of my love for Jesus, which comes through my faith in Him and the gift of healing. He uses me for His glory.

The greatest beginning of prayer is "our Father who is in heaven, how holy is Your name."

The Lord Holy God is gracious, grateful, generous, graceful, glorious, and good. He is the Lord of all. He came to give us light, life, and love through healing and holiness in Him.

The Lord does not give you what you want but what you need. That is His holy will and purpose: holy, holy, holy, Lord God Almighty.

Is there ever a time to pray? Of course the answer is yes; it is always time to pray, in crisis or in hope. This is certainly a crisis. We urgently need a time of praise and prayers.

Prayer, when it is utterly honest, will bring ultimate results for God's glory and truth.

Prayer passes the smell test. Its aroma is sweet to the soul and pleasing to the heart.

"And now unto Him who is able to keep that which we have committed unto Him against that day." He is the One who divides who we are and what we are.

What a difference a lot of prayer daily makes in our lives and the lives of our families.

God is in the spiritual business of saving souls and answering prayers in His will and time.

Prayer brings faith, which leads to hope. Lastly, it gives us love. These are the ingredients of a holy and helpful God, which lead to holiness.

Remember, prayer is used by God as we talk and listen to Him. From this interaction, many people change for the good. We are the bride of Christ. Our hope in Him gives us hope in ourselves.

Pray for our world and world leaders. Pray for our churches across the world, that those churches will deeply influence that world.

The Lord is in His holy temple 24/7, waiting on our call to Him.

Happy are those who trust the Lord and, in prayer, follow His teachings.

Prayer is answered when it is truthfully honest and sincerely thought out.

I believe in prayer more than ever before. Why? Because it has worked for me for eighty years, it is working for me right now, and it will continue working for me and for the many hundreds I pray with and for regularly.

We, the born again, are already covered by the blood of Jesus. What comes out of our mouths is filtered by the Holy Spirit. So masks on our faces are appropriate to filter what comes in and out of our mouths. The masks will remind us that what we say is actually coming from our hearts, as the Bible teaches. The Christian kid's song says, "Be careful what you say." On the other hand, the mask says, "Be careful for you and for others; God bless us all and help us all."

Prayer in the morning makes us strong for the day ahead. When we are ready for rest, prayer gets us ready for the next day.

Prayers, medical research, medication, rest, healthy living, faith in God, doctors' expertise, and hope bring healing. When all else fails, trust wholly in the prayer warriors in your church.

Sincere prayer will help greatly in healing sexual, drug, nicotine, and porn addictions. Do not count out using prayer. Prayer will counter all addictions with faith in God.

Do not hesitate to put prayer at the forefront of all your mental, physical, and spiritual needs.

Remember, prayer can heal a broken heart and a discouraged soul.

> Do not fear I am with you;
> Do not be dismayed,
> For i am your God.
> I will strengthen you and help you.
> I will uphold you with my righteous right hand. (Isaiah 41:10 NIV)

Why pray?

- God is listening.
- God loves you.
- God answers with His will and purpose.
- You need to prepare yourself for what is ahead in your life.
- Your spouse, family, and church need your prayers.

- You get saved by praying for forgiveness.
- Sick and defeated people need your prayers.
- Prayer is two-way, from you to God and from Him back to you.
- Prayer changes your wrong thoughts and desires to right thoughts toward Him and His will.

So why pray? It works for those who trust and obey.

There has been a huge battle in America for fifty-plus years. Those on one side actually believe prayer is useless. Those of us on the other side know and believe prayer works wonders and is the strength of life. We will not fail with God!

"My hope is built on nothing less than Jesus, His Blood and righteousness." Have you found Him by letting Him build in you His blood and righteousness? Just trust Him.

The devil steals, but God always heals.

Prayer changes the attitudes that are wrongfully a disruption to the good intentions in the heart.

The heart will not go weary when it is committed to God and His love and power. Always remember that God is the Lover of your soul.

God will always be there in your time of need and your place of disorder.

CHAPTER 7.

Prayer: Holy Days and Holidays

Easter
Today is no more sorrow.
Yesterday our hope was for tomorrow.
So hope has come,
And it is not just for some,
But for all who call upon His name.
Come, let us worship,
For He is risen as He said.

Bible Verses that Tell of the Holy Days

Today in the town of David a Savior has been born to you; He is Christ the Lord. (Luke 2:11 KJV)

Then Jesus said to them, "Do not be afraid. Go and tell my brothers to go to Galilee; there they will see me." (Matthew 28:10 KJV)

Testimonies and Stories that Tell about Christmas

A story is told of a large city's downtown Catholic cathedral the week before Christmas. The cathedral authorities purchased a new, gold-covered Baby Jesus to replace an older replica of the one in their manger scene in front of the building. On Christmas Eve, the bishop went out to check the manger in preparation for the midnight Mass. Everything just right—except that the Baby Jesus was missing. He quickly called the police, who immediately sent two officers to check that inner city neighborhood, trying to locate Jesus.

Two blocks from the cathedral, they noticed a little boy pulling a bright-red wagon down the sidewalk. Looking closer, they saw the shining Baby Jesus wrapped in a blanket placed in the wagon. They pulled over to the curb and asked the boy where he was going with the Baby Jesus. He told them that he had prayed for a new wagon for Christmas, and he had promised Jesus the first ride in it if Jesus answered his prayers.

That is quite a story for the Christmas season. It reminds me of my own prayer for a new, bright-red bicycle for my Christmas present when I was a boy. My parents were by no means wealthy at that time, so my dad bought an old bike and fixed it up to ride well. Then he painted it bright red for my surprise and excitement on Christmas morn.

As we get close to Christmas, let us make every day closer to Jesus. By Christmas, we will be closer than ever before to Him.

Prayer and Christmas go hand in hand. Put them together today and tomorrow. Pray and let God's power work. Merry Christmas.

Is saying "Merry Christmas "becoming more popular again? Are store decorations and personal Christmas greetings back in vogue? I think they are. I am for greetings of "Merry Christmas" again. Are you?

A Christmas thought: He is the wisest God of all gods, presented to us in His grace and glory.

"And now unto Him who is able, to keep that which I have committed unto Him against that day."

Now we remember the first coming of Jesus and anticipate His Second Coming. Now we remember His first coming at Christmas and praise the name of the Lord God Almighty.

It is time to stand up for Jesus. Why? Because it is the Christmas season, and thus the time to rejoice and be glad. So rejoice in the Lord at Christmas always, and again I say, "Rejoice."

I hope that on Christmas Eve, you go to the midnight candlelight service at your church and pray for yourself, your family, your church, your country, and the world. Spend that day of Christmas loving on your family and helping the needy.

Christmas is a holy day of the year when we praise God for sending us His Son to give us hope for eternal life. We call it Christmas. It stands for "Christ Mass," as the Catholic church identified it, having Mass on that day. It became tradition over the years to celebrate the Mass on Christmas Eve at around midnight, with a beautiful candlelight service celebrating the birthday of the Christ Child.

Christmas became so popular as a religious holy day that the greeting "Merry Christmas" became a staple for most people in the Christian tradition. The greeting lost its luster for some in recent years, especially in America, due to the emphasis on not offending those who do not believe in Christ. The most recent Christmas season seem to have seen a revival of the greeting.

Prayer and Christmas go hand in hand. Put them together today and tomorrow. Pray and let God's power work. Merry Christmas.

It is time to stand up for Jesus. Why? Because it is the Christmas season. It is the time to rejoice and be glad. Rejoice in the Lord always, and again I say, "Rejoice."

We have all committed sins and fall short of the glory of God. In His birth, we receive hope and victory over sin and even death. What a blessed hope!

The Christian year has several traditions. One is Christmas, the celebration of Christ and His birth two thousand years ago.

Another is Lent. The Lenten season begins on Ash Wednesday, when there is a special service in churches. Ashes are used to mark the sign of the cross, and prayers are made in preparation for Christ's death. The following six-week period of denial and sacrifice is celebrated with weekly church services on each Wednesday. Then comes Maundy Thursday, the day prior to the Friday of Christ's death, celebrated with a meal. Good Friday is the solemn day of remembering Christ's death. Noon to 3:00 p.m. is traditionally observed as the time of His suffering on the cross, with 3:00 p.m. His time of death. Two thousand years ago, Christ died for us, and that day was really bad. But after His coming back to life, that day has proven to mark His great victory over sin and death. This is why we call it Good Friday.

The Lenten season ends with Easter, the great time of celebration of His resurrection. For the believer, Easter represents our hope for forgiveness of sin and eternal life. We rejoice in the memory of Jesus dying for us and coming back to life. It is a great day of celebration and worship. The Lord is risen; yes, the Lord is risen indeed. Blessed be the name of the Lord.

> Palm Sunday
> A parade of the Light
> Bad Friday
> The pull of darkness
> Easter Sunday
> The power of the resurrection
> Happy Holy Week

This Holy Week, I believe in the death of Jesus and His subsequent resurrection. He did this for you and for me. Praise God.

While in the tomb, Jesus must have rested and prayed to prepare Himself for Easter. If you think He did great things before the tomb in this life, think about what happened after He rose. He went up to His far greater heavenly role, to even more powerful and great things, after His victory over sin and death. Praise God.

Folks, on Easter He rose and gave us the only hope over sin and death. He gave us the resurrection and its result, eternal life. He rose, and happy days are forever here.

> Today is no more sorrow,
> For yesterday our hope was for tomorrow.
> So hope has come,
> And it is not just for some,
> But for all who call upon His name.
> Come, let us worship.
> He has risen as He said.

> Folks...it's okay if the church is empty on Easter. The Tomb was empty
> too! (Country livin)

The six Sundays prior to Christmas are called Advent. Christians have weekly services to prepare for the coming of the Baby Jesus.

Holy Week is the seven days from Palm Sunday to Easter Sunday.

On other special days, how about thinking more about holiness and service to God, family, and church? A holiday is a great time to pray and seek holiness.

Martin Luther King Day

Martin Luther King preached great sermons for both blacks and whites in his lifetime in twentieth-century America. In his sermons about the kingdom of God and about how all men and women are created equal, he helped our country and the world of his day. He eventually died as a martyr for preaching the truth. He was one of a few who preached love, righteousness, and justice in a way that still echoes today. This holiday is a great day to honor him.

Memorial Day

Veterans are the heart of what makes America better. That includes those who suffered and those who made the ultimate sacrifice in all wars and all conflicts in all countries. I send out particular thanks to our veterans of the Vietnam War, where 58,000 service personnel died and many, many more suffered, including those who continue to suffer today.

Fourth of July

The Fourth of July is America's celebration of our victory over the British. We celebrate it every year with fireworks displays and picnic dinners. For probably more than two hundred years, we have celebrated, and one of our earlier presidents declared it a holiday. The churches eventually joined with the country to co-celebrate this country's celebration with their own prayers, picnics, and fireworks.

Veterans Day

On November 11 each year, we in America remember our veterans and thank them for their service. The greatest men and women of America are those who were and are willing to sacrifice body, mind, and spirit for our country. We thank you and pray for you.

Pray for the families of those lost in World War I, World War II, Korea, Vietnam, Afghanistan, Iran, and other conflicts. We thank You, God, for all who suffered and died, or who are still suffering. I offer particular thanks for the sacrifices incurred on December 7, 1941, when so many were lost.

Thanksgiving

Happy Thanksgiving to all on a day that is especially special to Americans. For Thanksgiving, let us thank God Almighty both morning and night. We should be giving thanks every day of the 365 a year, not just Thanksgiving Day. Thank You, Jesus.

D-Day

On this day, we can only think of love and prayer. We thank God for hope, help, and holiness. Thank You for the blood and treasure and for the sacrifice of many for the freedom of our country.

Mother's Day

Happy Mother's Day to all mothers everywhere. The song says, "Red and Yellow, Black and White, they are precious in His sight." The line comes from a children's song that can be applied to mothers. Happy Mother's Day to all the grandmothers, mothers, and wives who are mothers. We love you all and will always be blessed from and by you. God bless you all. And God bless the memories of all moms who have gone before us.

September 11

The numbers 9/11 remind the world of the collapse of the World Trade Center that caused the death of thousands, and the thousands of related deaths in the years that followed. What a sad commentary that day was on what one or two people cans do to destroy many people in a few seconds. God, help us to find these people before they do so again. Help suppress this evil mindset and bring the mind of Christ into the situation through the power of intense prayer.

Just remember that, in the time of disaster and need, God is good all the time, even when times are bad. Keep praying. "He will work all things together for good, for those of us who love him and know Him and are called according to His Purposes."

If there is a bad storm coming from out on the ocean, just pray for it to stay on the ocean. Just pray, and God will hear your prayers.

If you don't believe God, let me tell you what the Bible says: through our calling out to Him in a storm, He hears our prayers. There is a story in the Old Testament about Jonah and the large fish. There is another story about the Israelites and God's parting of the Red Sea so they could get away from their enemy. When their enemy started through that opening in the waters, the parting quickly closed and killed all the enemies. Yes, God hears our prayers.

When I pray for needs and tough times, the beginning of my prayer is "My Father in heaven, You are my Savior, Friend, and Helper." I end my prayer "in the strong name of Jesus. In the name of the Father, the Son, and the Holy Spirit."

What is the most important act we can do in something like the 9/11 crisis? This is a no-brainer. Yes, the answer is to stand firm on the Word of God through His power in Jesus Christ. So come on, prayer warriors! Let us pray and pray some more.

> And He saith unto them, Be not amazed: ye seek Jesus, the Nazarene, who hath been crucified: He is risen; He is not here.

> And now unto Him who is able to keep you from falling, and present you faultless before the presence of His Glory with exceeding joy. Unto the one and only true and wise God our Father, be Glory and Majesty, Dominion and power, both now and forever more. Amen.

More Testimonies and Stories about Holidays

I have two equally favorite holidays, and they are both Christian: Christmas and Easter. Receiving gifts on Christmas Eve and Christmas morning was always the highlight of my childhood. I was always excited about getting many gifts and opening them. As I became a teenager my understanding of gift-giving slowly began to change. I was a Christian and more deeply understood that God gave us the greatest gift in the person of His Son Jesus.

Good Friday brings back a different kind of memory. Years ago, there was a man in my church in Convoy, Ohio, named Brian Stewart. He had at one time auditioned in Nashville as a country-western singer. I do not know why he did not succeed, as in my mind he was a big star. He sang many times in my church while I was there and also for the preachers who followed me.

I went to the local barbershop one Good Friday, and all the regular customers were there. Brian was playing the guitar, and I have honestly never been to a better impromptu Good Friday service. Wow.

On Easter Sunday, I contemplate how Christ has risen as He said He would. In my childhood, He gave me hope for eternal life, which has carried me to the eternal hope I have today. He lives, and I know He lives within my heart.

On Mother's Day, let me emphasize the importance of mothers. Other than God and Christ, mothers are the most powerful force in our world. They are the heart of the home and the strength of all nations. Mothers are the second hope of the world. Happy Mother's Day to all of you.

CONCLUSION

Beginning my fifty-eighth year of ministry, I have learned much—through fear and trepidation, grace and divine love—about what ministry really is. I have learned what prayer is in me and in the lives of prayer warriors. I also have learned what the church really is. A building is only a part. The church is absolutely the people of God.

Even though I have not found true holiness, in the sense of what is traditionally meant in the Word and in the various methodologies of the holiness movement, I still seek it. Despite my lack of it, I keep looking for it in daily prayers and listening to God.

Today, I move forward in ministry, and there is no turning back nor detours. I hopefully and faithfully plow forward in this life and upward in the future, eternal life. The old song says, "Who will come and go with me? I am bound for the promised land."

With those thoughts, I share what God told me when I was seventy-six years old. He told me He was giving me ten years more of ministry. Following that revelation, I became very ill. I went to the hospital and was admitted into intensive care with sepsis, pneumonia, and influenza. After treatments that lasted six days, I returned home for a very slow year of recovery.

Soon after that recovery, during which my health improved immensely, I developed severe back pain. Since I have had several kidney stone attacks over my lifetime, I went to my specialist. After X-rays, he told me there were twenty-one stones inside me. I had never heard of someone having so many at once.

After a few surgeries, drinking tons of water, and another year of recovery, God told me to get to work on my ten-year calling. I told Him I only had eight years left after the two-year hiatus of illness. God told me I still had ten years of ministry. I immediately corrected Him, saying that I had already lived two years of the ten. To my amazement, He corrected my math by telling me that because I had been sick for two years, I still had ten to go. Do not argue with God.

So the ten years started one and one-half years ago, and here I am, finishing this book with eight and one-half years to live what it teaches. I hope to see many others use it too.

The interesting note to me is that He did not tell me what would happen to me after the ten years. All that is God's problem concerning His work on me, "a Christian still under construction."

I turn again to my four heroes, then earthly but now heavenly. First is Dr. Harold Dutt, under whom I was saved and called to preach when I was six years old. As a little kid, a boy, and a teen, I sat under his ministry. He was a man of God and taught me how to seek surrender for seventeen years.

I went with Dr. Dutt to meetings led by E. Stanley Jones in his spiritual retreat when I was fourteen and fifteen years old. It was there that I first heard about surrender and also about Asbury College and Seminary, from which both Dutt and Jones had graduated. This was all part of God's plan for my life.

What happens when fear tries to overcome faith? We all have felt the pull from these two directions. The only answer we know is "greater is He that within us than he who is in the world."

They that wait upon the Lord shall renew their strength, they shall mount
up their wings as eagles, they shall run and not be weary, and they shall
walk and not faint.

Some say, "Where is God in times of crisis or tragedy?" Do not fear. The Word says, "He will be never leave us nor forsake us."

Sometimes we wonder what will happen to us in this life. But if we trust in the Lord's Word and prayer, all will end well.

We can hide secrets from our closest friends or family about who we are as finite people. But we cannot hide any secrets from God, because He is infinite and knows and sees all. Therefore there is only one way to live: *surrender*. "All to Jesus I surrender, all to Him I freely give."

And now unto Him who is able to keep us from falling and present us
faultless before the presence of His Glory with exceeding Joy. Unto the
only wise God our Father, be Glory, and Majesty, Dominion and Power,
both now and forever more. Amen and Amen.

Had a powerful movie like a vision in the clouds last night.

Saw a window and it opened.

Then a large cross appeared.

Then Jesus was hanging on the cross in agony.

Next Jesus slumped.

Then He woke up and smiled like it was over.

Next, out of nowhere, a cloud formed as a round rock and rolled away from the large, bright opening.

Next I saw a tree limb looking like an angel. It was holding a halo over a man with a large crown on his head. But I looked again and the man was not a man, but a lion. After I thought about it for a minute, God said, "The lion of Judah." The angel of Judah had a bright blue light shining through his body.

That was the vision.

The king is coming.

"This is the end of the matter; all hath been heard; fear God." And pray like you never have before.

Printed in the United States
by Baker & Taylor Publisher Services